The Bride's Essential

Bridesmaid's Handbook

Savvy Advice, Sensational Showers,
and Secrets to Success

‿⁓ ⁓‿

Kathy Passero

Illustrations by Greg Stadler

Sterling Signature
NEW YORK

Sterling Signature
NEW YORK

An Imprint of Sterling Publishing
387 Park Avenue South
New York, NY 10016

This edition published in 2013 by Sterling Publishing Co., Inc.

ISBN 978-1-4549-0841-8

Distributed in Canada by Sterling Publishing
c/o Canadian Manda Group, 165 Dufferin Street
Toronto, Ontario, Canada M6K 3H6
Distributed in the United Kingdom by GMC Distribution Services
Castle Place, 166 High Street, Lewes, East Sussex, England BN7 1XU
Distributed in Australia by Capricorn Link (Australia) Pty. Ltd.
P.O. Box 704, Windsor, NSW 2756, Australia

For information about custom editions, special sales, and premium and corporate purchases, please
contact Sterling Special Sales at 800-805-5489 or specialsales@sterlingpublishing.com.

Manufactured in China

6 8 10 9 7 5

www.sterlingpublishing.com

*For Valerie, the best bridesmaid and the best friend
anyone could ever hope to have.*

Acknowledgments

I would like to express my gratitude to Melissa Abernathy, Alice Cary, Debby Carr, Lisa Chambers, Loren Edelstein, Monica Gruber, Kim Kozian, Jeanne O'Brien-Coffey, Rebecca Reisner, Eleni Shipe, Bernadette Starzee, and all the other veteran bridesmaids whose insights, experiences, and anecdotes contributed to this book. Thank you for sharing your wisdom and your war stories. I loved hearing all of them. Without your input this book would never have been possible. Thank you also to my very talented and patient editor, Hallie Einhorn; to my own long-suffering bridesmaids, Deb and Jody; to Greg, without whom I would not have had the chance to see bridesmaids from a bride's point of view; to Mom and Dad for reading every word (as always); and to my precious daughter, Darby, for understanding when I had to do research or write rather than watch Elmo.

Contents

Introduction

So you've been asked to be a bridesmaid. Congratulations! You've been given a highly special honor. The bride, a woman near and dear to your heart, has asked you to play a part in what is one of the most important days of her life. There will be parties to attend, shopping to do, and bonding moments to share. But, in addition to the fun and games, your role comes with responsibilities.

What lies ahead? One common frustration of being a bridesmaid is not knowing what to expect or what's expected of you. Who's supposed to be invited to the bridal shower? When should you buy your dress, and who pays? Are you required to attend all of the prewedding parties, and do you need to give a gift at each one? And how do you balance all of your bridesmaid duties with your own busy life?

In this book you'll find answers to these questions and many more. The following pages are filled with not only guidance and advice, but also loads of ideas for showers, bachelorette parties, and making the bride feel special. In addition, there are checklists, budget worksheets, planning timelines, and other practical tools designed to help make your role in the wedding easier. And there are insider tips from actual brides and bridesmaids, as well as savvy strategies for getting along with all of the players involved, saving money, and making your planning responsibilities run more smoothly.

Whether this is your first time being a bridal attendant or your tenth, this handbook can help you sail through the experience with grace and style. As you'll soon see, with a little guidance and the right attitude, anyone can be a sensational bridesmaid and have fun in the process.

Chapter One

More Than Just a Pretty Face
Bridesmaid Basics

When you're asked to be a bridesmaid, the first images that often spring to mind involve you and a group of grinning clones dressed in hideous matching outfits, standing beside a gorgeous bride and groom while a photographer clicks away, capturing the moment—and your lovely ensemble—for eternity. To the uninitiated, bridal attendants might seem primarily ornamental, but there's much more to them than that. Bridesmaids have always played a vital role in protecting the bride and ensuring her happiness. Once upon a time, they stood by her to protect her from physical harm. Today, the protection they offer pertains more to the bride's emotional state. They shower the bride with love and encouragement as well as moral and practical support. This can involve fielding panicked phone calls at midnight, racing to the drugstore to pick up a last-minute package of tampons, or raising a flute of champagne and telling a roomful of warm, glowing faces what a special place this woman holds in your heart.

Checklist of Responsibilities

The following checklist outlines the traditional responsibilities of bridal attendants. Those duties usually performed by the maid of honor appear in italics. Please note that these are general guidelines only; depending on the type of wedding, the bride's specific needs, your personal situation, and the situations of the other attendants, you may be called upon to do more or less. Also note that those responsibilities traditionally assigned to the maid of honor may be handled by other attendants.

Prewedding Period
- ❏ Attend the engagement party, if it's within a reasonable distance
- ❏ Buy an engagement present (optional if you haven't been invited to an engagement party)
- ❏ Help the bride shop for her wedding gown, if she so desires
- ❏ *Attend the bride's gown fitting to learn how to bustle the train, if applicable*
- ❏ Help the bride shop for bridesmaid dresses, if she so desires
- ❏ Show up for your bridesmaid dress fittings, if you're local
- ❏ Pay for your own bridesmaid dress, shoes, and accessories
- ❏ Arrange and pay for your accommodations and transportation to the wedding
- ❏ Obtain a wedding present for the bride and groom
- ❏ *Take the lead in organizing the bridal shower*
- ❏ Work with the other attendants to plan and pay for the bridal shower
- ❏ Purchase a shower present
- ❏ Attend the bridal shower
- ❏ *Provide the bride with a record of who gave what gifts at the shower*
- ❏ Work with the other bridesmaids/friends of the bride to plan and pay for the bachelorette party
- ❏ Buy a bachelorette party present (optional)
- ❏ Attend the bachelorette party
- ❏ Attend the bridesmaids' luncheon, if one is held
- ❏ Step in at the bride's request to assist in any reasonable way you can with the

wedding planning process (address and/or assemble invitations, help select favors, etc.)
- ❑ Lend a sympathetic ear and act as a sounding board for the bride
- ❑ Provide all-around emotional and moral support for the bride
- ❑ Communicate and coordinate with the other bridesmaids on wedding-related issues
- ❑ Maintain an upbeat, positive, cooperative attitude
- ❑ Be tactful, patient, and nonjudgmental

Wedding Whirlwind
- ❑ Assist with any last-minute crises that arise
- ❑ Attend the rehearsal and rehearsal dinner
- ❑ Make a toast at the rehearsal dinner (optional)
- ❑ Attend any other wedding-related events
- ❑ Run last-minute errands and perform last-minute tasks at the request of the bride (arrange place cards and table numbers, put up signs directing guests to the reception, place favors on the tables, etc.)
- ❑ Attend and pay for professional makeup and hair appointments, if applicable
- ❑ Help the bride get dressed on the wedding day
- ❑ Come prepared with an "emergency wedding kit" that contains items such as a sewing kit, asprin, hair pins, stain remover, extra panty hose, extra earring backs, static cling spray, and hair spray.
- ❑ Pose for formal portraits (this may occur before or after the ceremony)
- ❑ Maintain a cheerful, positive, enthusiastic attitude whenever dealing with the bride, bridal party, guests, and/or vendors
- ❑ Keep the bride calm, making sure she has privacy and quiet time if needed

Ceremony
- ❑ Walk down the aisle and stand up with the bride during the ceremony
- ❑ *Straighten the bride's train and veil immediately after the processional*

- ❑ *Carry the groom's ring, and hand it to the bride at the appropriate moment for the ring exchange*
- ❑ *Hold the bride's bouquet during the ceremony, and return it to her for the recessional*
- ❑ *Sign the marriage license, if asked to do so*
- ❑ Perform any end-of-ceremony tasks requested by the bride (collect the unity candle, transport floral arrangements from the ceremony to the reception site, etc.)

Reception

- ❑ Stand in the receiving line, if asked to do so (this can take place at the ceremony site instead)
- ❑ Be as helpful as possible (assist guests in finding the coat check, restroom, bar, or correct table number; introduce guests to one another; encourage them to sign the guest book)
- ❑ *Bustle the bride's train*
- ❑ *Help the bride with her dress when she needs to use the ladies' room*
- ❑ Participate in a wedding party dance, if asked to do so
- ❑ Make a toast, if applicable
- ❑ Stay sober and ready to help resolve any problems that arise
- ❑ Dance with guests in need of a partner, encourage others to boogie, and participate in group dances (hora, tarantella, conga line, etc.) and the bouquet toss
- ❑ Perform any tasks requested of you by the bride (guide the photographer to important people to photograph; collect the guest book, cake topper, disposable cameras, or other items at the end of the event)

❑ *Help the bride change into her going-away outfit, if applicable*

❑ *At the bride's request, take her wedding gown home or to the dry cleaner that she has selected*

❑ Help with the transportation of wedding gifts after the reception

REFLECTIONS FROM REAL BRIDES

"I had an interesting job as a bridesmaid for my friend Jeannine. Her dress had layers upon layers of tulle underneath, a petticoat kind of thing, and it was an outdoor wedding on a blazing hot and humid day with temperatures in the 90s. Not only did I have to hold her dress up for her when she needed to go to the bathroom, but it was also my job to periodically duck into the dressing room with a blow-dryer and blow cool air up the dress to cool her down! Now, that's a friend!**"**

—LOREN G. EDELSTEIN

The Maid of Honor

❋ First, a word about words. Technically, the phrase "maid of honor" refers to a single woman, while "matron of honor" refers to a married one. That said, the term "maid of honor" is commonly used regardless of the individual's marital status, as it is in this book. This special member of the wedding party can also be referred to as an honor attendant.

❋ Usually the bride's dearest friend or sibling, the maid of honor naturally serves as the bride's closest confidante.

❋ The maid of honor traditionally acts as the primary host and organizer of the bridal shower and the bachelorette party and serves as the point person for the other bridesmaids. She also performs special tasks on the wedding day, as indicated in the preceding checklist.

Cents and Sensibility

The amount you spend as a bridesmaid will vary tremendously depending on geographic region and the type of wedding the bride and groom are planning. That said, it's best to realize up front that being a bridesmaid is rarely an inexpensive undertaking. It's unlikely that you'll shell out less than $500; in fact, there's a good chance that the tab will be a lot higher. The endeavor becomes even pricier if you'll need to travel. Below is a general, comprehensive worksheet that you can use to plan ahead and keep track of your spending. (For details on the specific costs associated with throwing a bridal shower and bachelorette party, refer to pages 85 and 102, respectively.)

EXPENSE	ESTIMATED	ACTUAL
PARTIES		
Shower (cost of cohosting)		
Bachelorette party (cost of cohosting)		
Subtotal		
PRESENTS		
Engagement gift (optional if you haven't been invited to an engagement party)		
Shower gift		
Bachelorette party gift (optional)		
Wedding gift		
Group gift with other bridesmaids (optional)		
Subtotal		

EXPENSE	ESTIMATED	ACTUAL
ATTIRE		
Dress		
Alterations		
Shipping		
Shoes (including cost to dye them,		
if applicable)		
Lingerie		
Accessories		
Subtotal		
BEAUTY		
Hair		
Makeup		
Manicure/pedicure		
Subtotal		
TRAVEL (for parties and wedding)		
Transportation to and from destination		
Local transportation within wedding locale		
Rental car		
Accommodations		
Hostess gift (if you're staying with someone)		
Meals, activities, etc.		
Subtotal		
MISCELLANEOUS		
Other		
Other		
Other		
Other		
TOTAL		

SAFETY IN NUMBERS

THE TRADITION OF THE BRIDE HEADING TO THE ALTAR accompanied by a procession of women traces its roots back to ancient Greece. In that society, it was customary for a group of respected married women with children to surround the naive young bride on her way to her wedding in the hope that the mothers' fertility and good fortune would bring her luck and protect her from evil spirits.

The Time Factor

With all of the parties, shopping, and manicures, being a bridesmaid can be a lot of fun. But the role can involve a significant time commitment on your part. Precisely how much—and how taxing you'll find it—depends on the bride's personality and her approach to wedding planning. Some brides are so easygoing that you'll have little to do until just before the wedding. Others will want your advice on every single detail from the outset. You can probably get some idea of the time investment that lies ahead based on what you already know of your friend's personality. Ask yourself the following questions.

1. **How supportive does the bride expect you to be in general in your friendship?** Does she often ask for your advice and input?

2. **How involved have you been in the bride and groom's relationship up to this point?** If she's in the habit of giving you the play-by-play or asking you to analyze her honey's every move, you can expect to log some serious hours leading up to her wedding. If she didn't mention her engagement until weeks after the fact, you probably won't have to field too many late-night calls, though you may find it difficult to get the basic information you need from her.

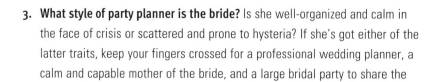

3. **What style of party planner is the bride?** Is she well-organized and calm in the face of crisis or scattered and prone to hysteria? If she's got either of the latter traits, keep your fingers crossed for a professional wedding planner, a calm and capable mother of the bride, and a large bridal party to share the load.

4. **How involved is the groom likely to be in planning the wedding?** If he gets a glazed look whenever the bride talks about registering for china and asks which teams are playing in the "Dessert Bowl," expect her to rely on you to muster enthusiasm for details like cake frostings and party favors. Likewise, if she tends to vent to you about the slightest dispute with the groom, brace yourself for plenty of counseling sessions, as wedding planning often tests the limits of even the most devoted and compatible couples.

5. **How involved are the families likely to be?** If they're beyond supportive (read controlling or interfering), she may need an unbiased outsider like yourself as a sounding board. If they're not involved enough, she may need to lean on you more.

6. **How many other bridesmaids are in the party, and what is the bride's relationship with them?** Are they all close pals or are some the groom's siblings, with whom the bride is not quite comfortable? If she's close to all of you, she'll probably divvy up wedding tasks and crisis calls so that no one feels put upon.

TIME TIP

TAKE A LOOK DOWN THE ROAD AT WHAT YOUR OWN SCHEDULE—personal and professional—has in store for you and plan accordingly; don't let yourself be blindsided. For instance, if you're a tax accountant and the bride is planning a May wedding, you know you're in for a hectic spring. Inform the bride and the other bridesmaids as early as possible about which weeks you'll be unavailable so that no one feels suddenly abandoned. Offer to take charge of responsibilities that fall during a quieter time in return for being able to bow out of others that need addressing during your crunch period. Plot out as much as you can in advance so that you don't feel overwhelmed and resentful later.

New Twists on Tradition

Times change and etiquette evolves. Today, guidelines regarding the members of the bridal party are more flexible than they used to be, resulting in situations that once upon a time were unheard-of.

The right man for the job: These days brides and grooms invite their closest friends and relatives, regardless of gender, to stand beside them at their wedding ceremony. Thus, terms such as "best person," "man of honor," "bridesman," and "groomswoman" have emerged in wedding speak. A male member of the bride's party walks down the aisle with the bridesmaids and stands with them on the bride's side. Likewise, a female member of the groom's party stands on the groom's side. If the bride has a male honor attendant, he will take charge of the groom's ring during the ceremony, just as a maid of honor would do; similarly, if the groom has a female honor attendant, she will be responsible for the bride's ring.

Good odds: In the past, couples often struggled to pare down their desired attendant roster or drum up a few more names to ensure even pairings of bridesmaids
and groomsmen. Today, bridal parties are often mismatched, which simply means
one groomsman may escort two bridesmaids during the recessional or vice versa.
Or the bride and groom may have the attendants walk solo and forgo traditional
wedding party dances.

Seeing double: For brides with a sister and a best friend, having two honor
attendants sometimes proves the best route. A bonus for the women in question:
The burden is lighter on each. It's up to the bride or the threesome to decide who
handles which of the traditional maid of honor duties.

Special Considerations

There are certain situations that can understandably affect a woman's involvement
as a bridesmaid. Such circumstances can have an impact on the other bridesmaids
and/or on the bride's own plans.

The Pregnant Bridesmaid

※ If you've signed on to be a bridesmaid and discover that you're expecting,
you should let the bride know as soon as possible since this development
will obviously affect her plans (if you've decided to wait until after the first
trimester to share the good news, make sure she's among the first you tell).
Discuss your role in the planning process, including any limitations you foresee
in terms of your ability to be involved. The fewer attendants the bride has, the
more important it is to talk about these issues early on.

※ If attending the wedding will require you to travel by plane, consult your
obstetrician; some don't want their patients to fly in the first or last trimester—
or to go out of town or engage in any activity that might raise the expectant
mom's blood pressure in the last month of pregnancy. Even if your doctor is

willing to let you fly, he/she may want you to follow certain rules about food and tap water if you're traveling abroad.

※ If travel issues are not preventing you from serving as a bridesmaid, consider whether you'll have enough energy to give to the bride. Also take into account the fact that you'll have many of your own preparations to take care of with a baby on the way; you may feel as though you've got too much on your plate and opt to bow out gracefully. Again, be up front with the bride. She may just be happy to have you stand beside her during the ceremony—even if you're not able to participate in the planning and other events.

※ If you need to excuse yourself from being a bridesmaid, don't wait. Explain your reasons, and thank the bride as graciously as you can.

※ If you do stay on as a bridesmaid, know that as a pregnant woman, you're well within your rights to refuse doing certain favors for the bride; don't do anything that might affect your well-being. Your health comes first.

※ Inquire about the length of the ceremony; if you can't remain standing that long, tell the bride. Perhaps you can sit in the front row with her family.

※ For information on what to wear, see page 58.

The Engaged Bridesmaid

※ Standing up for a friend when you know you'll be the next one at the altar is a mixed blessing. On the downside, you're making a commitment to help her plan her wedding when you're undoubtedly more interested in your own. On the upside, you get a free trial run and an insider's view of what to do, what to avoid, what can go wrong, and how to troubleshoot.

※ Consider how much time and energy you'll need to devote to planning your own wedding and whether you think you'll have any to spare. Making the preparations for your own wedding can often seem like a full-time job—and if you already have one of those, there may be little left to go around. Depending on your friend's expectations and how many other helpers she has, you could end up overcommitted.

❈ Make sure that the two wedding dates are not so close together that taking time out to attend hers would make pulling yours off too difficult.

❈ Have a heart-to-heart with the bride. Tell her at the outset how honored you are that she asked you to be a bridesmaid and how much her friendship means to you. Find out how involved she wants you to be, and speak honestly about any concerns you have.

❈ If you decide to decline, tell the bride that you care about her too much to shortchange her. Thank her for asking you to be a part of her wedding party, and assure her that if the timing had been different you would have loved to serve as her bridesmaid.

The Bridesmaid with Children

❈ Find out whether the bride intends to invite children to the wedding.

❈ If your kids are invited and you're considering bringing them, ask yourself whether your attention will be too divided to allow you to fulfill your duties as a bridesmaid. Remember, you're on call during the wedding and the hours leading up to it. When the bride asks you to run out to buy ribbon at the last minute, will your first urge be to refuse because your toddler might start to bawl the moment you leave? If such a conflict of interest seems likely but you're unwilling to leave the kids behind, talk the matter over with the bride. If she still wants you to participate, maybe you can take charge of prewedding events while the other women in the party serve as pinch hitters at the wedding itself.

❈ If your children are young, before deciding whether or not to bring them, find out how formal the event is and what time it ends. How many hours past your children's bedtime will that be? Keeping young kids up past their bedtime can be a recipe for disaster, and you don't want a major temper tantrum to disrupt the festivities.

❈ If you're married, have a discussion with your spouse about taking charge of the kids due to your limited availability during the wedding weekend. Make sure your kids understand that you'll be very busy, too.

❋ Find out if the bride has already made plans to accommodate guests with children. Some couples hire a professional baby-sitter at a nearby hotel where wedding guests are staying or enlist responsible teenage guests to oversee a children's table stocked with toys and games.

❋ If the wedding isn't local and you'd like to hire a baby-sitter but the bride hasn't offered any information, you can call the hotel where you'll be staying and ask for its list of recommended qualified sitters. You might also ask bridesmaids who have children and live in the area for referrals.

❋ Find out well in advance whether or not your kids will be invited to the rehearsal dinner so that you can make any necessary arrangements for a baby-sitter for that night, too. Rehearsal dinners are usually casual enough for a child to fit in, though they often run late.

❋ If you'd like to bring your children to the rehearsal itself, ask the bride. Keep in mind that if you bring them, you'll need someone to watch them, as you and the rest of the wedding party will be otherwise occupied.

❋ If you have teenagers, keep an eye on them at the open bar or have your spouse do so.

The Allergic Bridesmaid

❋ If you're allergic to certain cosmetics or flowers, let the bride know early in the planning stages of the wedding. While she's got a million other details to worry about, she'll be as miserable as you if the narcissus in your bouquet causes you to have a sneezing fit in the middle of her vows.

❋ If you're allergic to makeup or hairspray and the bride has scheduled professional beauty services, get the stylist's phone number and consult with him/her ahead of time. Find out whether he/she stocks hypoallergenic products or if you can bring your own and simply have them applied on the wedding day. If you're worried about a specific product, politely but firmly refuse it.

❋ If you have hay fever or other seasonal allergies, remember to take your usual medication. And come equipped with plenty of tissues just in case. If your medication makes you drowsy, ask your doctor for a different prescription far enough in advance of the event that you'll be able to give it a trial run. Also, if you take allergy medicine, follow the doctor's/pharmacist's instructions regarding alcohol intake.

Matters of Faith

※ If you're not of the same faith as the couple and they're planning a religious ceremony, you may want to ask the bride whether your abstinence from certain rituals, such as Communion, will pose a problem.

※ Know that you are not obligated to participate in any religious ritual with which you're not comfortable.

※ If you're not familiar with the religion, you may want to do a little research (at the library or on the Internet) so that you'll have a better idea of what to expect at the ceremony. You may also try to find a quiet moment to ask the bride directly.

All About Gifts

Which occasions am I supposed to buy gifts for? It's easy to feel like a personal shopper when you're a bridesmaid. Plan on giving a shower present and, of course, a wedding gift. If you're invited to an engagement party, you'll probably want to give a modest gift for that occasion. On top of all this, there's sometimes a group gift from the bridesmaids. Presents aren't usually given at a bachelorette party unless they're small tokens or gag gifts.

How much am I supposed to spend on gifts? Excluding bachelorette party gifts, which are usually small and often given as a group if they're given at all, the rule of thumb is to spend an increasing amount as the wedding approaches. One guideline is to double what you spend for each event from engagement to shower to wedding. In other words, if you pay $25 for an engagement gift, you pay $50 for a shower gift and

$100 for the wedding present. The amount spent on wedding gifts generally ranges from $50 to $200, depending on personal finances and geographic region.

What if I'm invited to more than one bridal shower? You only need to bring a gift to the first one.

What's this I'm hearing about a group gift, and do we have to give one? In addition to giving individual gifts, some bridesmaids present a joint gift to the bride. This type of present can be something small and personal, such as a nice photo album outfitted with pictures of the bridesmaids with the bride from throughout the years, or you can all chip in for something larger, such as jewelry or a silver tray engraved with her wedding date; it is usually presented at the bridal shower, the bridesmaids' luncheon, or the wedding itself. While a thoughtful gesture, such a present is by no means a requirement.

Must I buy something listed on the registry? No, though you should tailor whatever you select to the bride's tastes and needs. If she's registered only for casual tableware, don't buy her crystal candlesticks just because you think every newlywed needs them. And don't regift.

Can I go in on a wedding gift with another bridesmaid or two?

By all means. The advantage of this approach is that you'll be able to spring for something with a higher price tag—one of those dream items on the registry that few guests would consider buying. The drawback can be getting the other bridesmaids to reimburse you if you lay out the cash, especially if you don't know them that well. Your best bet is collecting the money up front or getting the participants to go shopping together—with their wallets.

Can I offer to do something in lieu of buying a gift?

Sure. If you're a gifted amateur photographer, you might offer your services for a bridal portrait, which the bride could use for newspaper announcements. If you're a fabulous baker whose sugar cookies the bride has always adored, she might be thrilled at your offer to bake heart-shaped treats personalized with the couple's

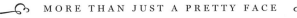

initials as favors. (A number of websites specializing in wedding favors sell tiny decorative canisters and tins that can be personalized, too.) Just be sure to find out if she's already made plans for the service before offering, as you don't want her to feel guilty about rejecting your proposed gift or pressured into changing her plans. Keep in mind that as a member of the wedding party, you won't be able to play videographer or photographer on the wedding day itself.

Can I make a gift? You can, if it's something truly special that comes from your heart and that you think the bride would love. If you're a world-class knitter, for example, you could make her an afghan in the colors she and the groom have chosen for their living room.

Do I have to bring the gift with me? You do not need to bring the wedding present to the wedding (in fact, it will probably be easier on you and the couple if you don't). Instead, you can send the present to the bride's home ahead of time. In fact, if you're purchasing a gift off the registry, the store will probably ship the item for you (for a fee) to an address provided by the bride. For a shower, you should arrive with your gift in hand, since the bride will most likely be opening her presents at the event (make sure to dress up the package with some ribbon or a bow that can be incorporated into a "ribbon bouquet" [see page 94]). If you can't attend the shower, ask the hostess if you can send it to her home so that it will be there when the bride arrives and it can be opened during the party (don't send it to the bride's home if the shower is a surprise). If you're going to an engagement party, it's best to bring the gift with you—provided that the invitation hasn't specified "no gifts," in which case you're off the hook.

Above and Beyond: Thoughtful Touches the Bride Is Bound to Love

※ Get the bride a subscription to a wedding magazine. (Do this early on, and make sure the magazine sends her a card informing her of the gift.)

※ Send the happy couple a bottle of wine from the year they met or started dating along with a card telling them how honored you are to be a part of their wedding.

※ Present the bride with a coupon for a specific service: an hour of tea and sympathy (advice optional), one girls' night out, one girls' night in, and so on. (Use the coupons at the back of this book, or make your own based on the bride's tastes.)

REFLECTIONS FROM REAL BRIDES

❝When I got engaged, one of my bridesmaids sent a beautiful bouquet of hydrangeas and roses to me at my office; she told me she did so not only to say 'congratulations,' but also to make sure that everyone at work would know my happy news. I was so in love with the arrangement that I ended up modeling the centerpieces for the reception after it. ❞

—ELIZABETH BECK

Chapter Two

Style and Savvy
How to Be a Great Bridesmaid and Have a Great Time

Bridesmaids are the unsung heroines of countless weddings. Some calm a nervous bride by making her break into laughter moments before she walks down the aisle. Others dance with all seven of the groom's balding, bachelor uncles. And still others save the day by finding a party rental supplier to set up a tent for an outdoor reception as an unanticipated storm suddenly approaches. Beyond an understanding of the basic responsibilities you're supposed to handle (review the checklist in chapter one if you're still fuzzy), your success as an ideal attendant boils down to your attitude and approach. Be an unwavering, unselfish friend. Pitch in cheerfully whenever you're needed. And be ready to roll with the punches when plans go awry. To have a great time in the process, simply resolve to have fun and refuse to let anything dampen your spirits.

"Bridesmaiding" for Beginners: Ten Strategies for Success

1. **Listen to the bride.** That doesn't just mean nodding patiently and patting her hand while she complains about how irrational her future in-laws are. It means paying attention to cues about what she wants from you. Remember that she's probably stress out with this wedding stuff, and she may not be able to articulate her needs precisely. Does she seem overwhelmed by the thought of finding a gown? Offer to help her make appointments at bridal salons and spend a day shopping with her (you can even volunteer to drive). If she's planning a non-traditional wedding where the bridesmaids wear what they like and guests mingle over cocktails, she probably doesn't want to pore over details, so don't bombard her with questions about what style of bouquet she's planning or what kind of music will be playing at the reception.

2. **Make an effort to get along with everyone.** That includes the other bridesmaids, the groom, the bride's mom, and all of the other major players. Do whatever you can to foster a spirit of cooperation, no matter what you really think of these people. Try to see matters from their point of view. If you're at your wits' end, remember that it will soon be over and you'll probably never have to spend an hour in the same room with these people again.

3. **Keep your opinions and your ego in check.** If you're dumbfounded that the bride wants to do the chicken dance at her reception, bite your tongue. If you've been outvoted on the shower theme, make the best of it. Being a team player means putting up with other people's decisions now and then. Be as open-minded and nonjudgmental as possible.

4. **Be a master of discretion.** Don't gossip with or about anyone involved in the wedding. If the bride tells you how many face-lifts her future mother-in-law has had, keep it to yourself—even if sharing this tidbit would help you bond with the other women in the party. If someone bad-mouths another bridesmaid, steer

the conversation in a different direction or listen politely without commenting. If you must vent, spill it to someone who doesn't know the couple and is unlikely ever to meet them. (Caveat: If you're griping about the bride's incessant wedding prattle, keep it brief; make sure you're not bending your confidante's ear just as the bride has been bending yours.)

5. **Be reliable.** If you promise to do something, do it. (Use the tips that start on page 34 to help you get organized, delegate responsibility, and manage your time.) If the bride or the other bridesmaids are setting goals or making requests you consider unrealistic, tell them so honestly but politely, and find a way to resolve the matter.

6. **Stay calm.** Unexpected events happen at weddings all the time. Buttons pop. Grooms faint. Cakes collapse. A great bridesmaid is resourceful and capable of changing gears quickly without losing her Zen-like demeanor. In the blink of an eye, she'll snatch the bride's veil out of a candle flame or step up to the microphone and wing a toast when the best man becomes paralyzed with stage fright (yes, this is your chance to be a superhero).

7. **Focus on your friendship.** Prop up a favorite photo of you and the bride on your dresser and another one by your phone. When your patience with her is wearing thin, glance at these images to help you keep things in perspective. Remind yourself that she's under a lot of pressure, and try to be understanding. Think about how you'd want her to behave if she were in your dyeable silk shoes and you were in her ivory ones.

8. **Set limits.** The bride's whole life may have been turned upside down or put on hold by this wedding, but that doesn't mean yours should be. Yes, you should be a sympathetic, supportive friend, but you don't have to cancel Friday night dates with the man in your life to help her pick out formalwear for the one in hers. Recognize when to draw the line to save your own sanity and to prevent resentment from building.

9. **Have a sense of humor.** Be willing to laugh at yourself and everything that's happening. So what if you have to wear a giant bow across your butt that makes you look like a walking Christmas present? So what if the groom's fifteen-year-old nephew won't stop hitting on you? It may make prime material for that best-selling novel you've been meaning to write (just be sure to change the names to protect the innocent).

10. **Enjoy yourself.** If you're miserable, it will show. Resolve not to let anyone or anything—including your outfit—get in the way of your walking away with happy memories of your friend's big day.

Survival Tactics: You and the Bride

Most brides are rational, reasonable people. In fact, a huge number of bridesmaids are pleasantly surprised to discover that their responsibilities are fewer and easier than they ever dreamed. However, if your friend seems to be turning into some monstrous new being you hardly recognize, the following tactics should help you preserve your peace of mind and your independence.

✳ If she's taking up hours and hours of your free time with wedding-related calls, let your answering machine pick up and call her back at a time that's more convenient for you. Try not to wait more than twenty-four hours to return the call, though. And if it sounds like a true emergency, get back to her right away.

※ Another solution to the problem of the loquacious bride is to schedule a weekly lunch or telephone gabfest and resign yourself to spending those hours as a sounding board (most wireless plans offer free night and weekend minutes). To make phone time more productive, get a headset (an inexpensive purchase) and multitask by performing some mindless chores—ones that won't take your concentration away from the bride.

※ If you think that the bride's behavior or requests are irrational, find a nonthreatening way to discuss the issue with her honestly and openly. Don't hold your tongue only to explode in a fit of anger or disappoint her later. If she's talking about having the entire bridal party splurge on $500 dresses and fly to Scotland for the wedding, gently explain that as much as everyone adores her and wants to share in her celebration, you suspect her plans might be beyond the means of most of the bridesmaids. Whenever possible, try to offer a helpful, thoughtful solution. In a situation like the one described above, you could ask to see a photograph of the expensive dresses she's set her heart on, and find a similar, more affordable alternative. If she's calling on a daily basis to rant about the groom, encourage her to talk matters out with him directly. Tell her that you think they're a lovely couple and that you care deeply about their happiness. Remind her that wedding planning is stressful for every couple who goes through it and that by working through differences, she and her honey will only strengthen their already rock-solid relationship.

Two persons cannot long be friends if they cannot forgive each other's little failings.

— Jean de la Bruyère

Wrestling with Your Own Emotions

Sometimes the problem lies not with the bride but with the bridesmaid. Let's face it: Watching a close friend tie the knot can stir up a whole range of emotions. And it can happen regardless of whether you're married or single. Below are a few common dilemmas, as well as hints for handling them.

The friendship is changing: Either her personality seems different or the dynamic in your relationship has shifted. Either way, you feel you hardly recognize this woman you've known for years. First, realize that the change is probably temporary. She's got a lot on her mind, and she's trying to adjust to a new role in her life and her family (not to mention his). She'll probably snap back to the friend you know and adore right after the honeymoon. If you're in doubt, take comfort in the fact that you're putting yourself out as a bridesmaid to honor the years you've spent as pals. Just be yourself and hopefully you'll coax her true personality out of hiding sooner or later.

Always-a-bridesmaid syndrome: Too many bridesmaids fall victim to the self-pity trap. Remember that this event is not about you. Keep your focus on the bride, and keep your own emotions out of her wedding. The fact that your best friend found Mr. Right doesn't diminish your own chances. Who knows? You might even meet him at the reception . . .

Jealousy: The green-eyed monster is an uninvited guest at many a wedding. A married bridesmaid sometimes envies the excitement and attention a new bride is enjoying. A single one sometimes thinks that if she had only met the groom first, *she* would be the one wearing white. When it comes to friendships that have always included a bit of rivalry, competitive feelings can be heightened, but follow the advice for "always-a-bridesmaid syndrome" and keep your mind on the bride. Also, give yourself a little treat after every major hurdle to boost your morale.

Resentment: You're spending a fortune on this wedding and the bride hasn't uttered so much as a thank-you. Remember that she's exceedingly busy and trying to keep track of a thousand details. She appreciates what you're doing even if she isn't showing it right now. It's a little like those movie award winners who thank the key grip and the coffee guy but forget to mention their spouse. Chances are the bride will shower you with gratitude after the wedding, when her head's clear again. If your resentment stems from overextending yourself, you need to establish some boundaries. Limit the time you're spending with the bride, or hand off some duties to the other attendants.

Control issues: You can't bear the fact that the bride—your friend from culinary class—is knuckling under and letting the groom's weakness for mini-weenies and mozzarella sticks set the tone for the hors d'oeuvres (he probably calls them "apps"). One of a bridesmaid's most indispensable skills is knowing when to relax, back off, and reserve judgment. If the bride has traded mermaids' purses (caviar in puff pastry) for pigs in a blanket, she's got her reasons. Accept her choice and move on. It's her wedding, not yours.

Message for the Maid of Honor

BEING ASKED TO PLAY SUCH AN IMPORTANT ROLE in one of the biggest days of the bride's life is truly a special honor. It says a great deal about how much she thinks of you and treasures your friendship. As the bride's right-hand woman, you should be prepared to put in significantly more time and TLC than the other bridesmaids. Resist any urge you might feel to compare the demands she's putting on you to what she's expecting from the other attendants, the groom, or her family. In most cases, the bulk of the prewedding party planning will be yours, so use the tips starting on page 34 to get organized and be as productive as possible.

Getting Organized

One of the best things you can do for yourself as a bridesmaid is to be efficient. That means getting organized and budgeting your time. Doing so will save you from countless hours of frustration and help you to maintain your sanity.

Details, Details! How to Master Them Without Losing Your Mind

1. Create a wedding organizer. All you need is a three-ring binder with some hole-punched, lined notebook paper and clear plastic pockets that you can use for storing notes and magazine clippings. Keep everything related to the wedding in this binder. That way you won't waste valuable time searching for papers, and you'll be able to put your hands on what you need quickly.

2. Compile a mini-directory of all important wedding-related contact information. You can create your own or use the removable guided directory that starts on page 149 and fill in the specifics.

3. As early as possible, talk to the bride about what you can do to help so that you have plenty of notice and can budget your time.

4. If you don't know the other bridesmaids, make contact with them (a friendly phone call or e-mail will do for starters). Gauge how dependable and involved they'll be and how easily you'll be able to work together. (For specific tips on dealing with challenging personalities, see page 40.)

5. Divvy up responsibilities among the bridesmaids. The maid of honor usually delegates, but if another bridesmaid is a born leader and organizer, there's no reason she can't take charge, provided the maid of honor doesn't object.

Time Management Tips

1. Put a clock by your phone and watch your talk time. Keep calls to the other bridesmaids friendly but short and focused. If necessary, put a timer by the phone and start it as soon as you begin a conversation. Not only will this device help you monitor the minutes, it will give you a polite excuse to hang up (when the buzzer sounds, tell the person on the other end that you've got something on the stove or that someone's at the door).

2. If one of the bridesmaids is a rambling conversationalist who keeps you on the phone for hours, resolve to communicate with her by e-mail only.

3. Create a new e-mail group in your computer's address book that includes all of the other bridesmaids so you can easily send notes and updates to everyone at once.

4. Set aside a certain time block every week to tackle wedding-related projects. Decide ahead of time which tasks you'll work on each week, then adhere to your list and allotted time frame as strictly as you can. Put your bridesmaid responsibilities out of your mind until then, and be firm about wrapping them up on schedule.

5. Don't procrastinate. Doing so only prolongs the agony.

6. Whenever a specific task seems too overwhelming to tackle, try the Swiss cheese method—punch little holes in it. In other words, focus on finishing small pieces of it at a time rather than taking care of enormous chunks or the entire project at once.

Instant Stress Relievers

1.　Put a favorite upbeat song on the stereo, crank up the volume, and sing and dance. You'll release frustration and experience a rush of mood-boosting endorphins. Bonus: If you catch sight of yourself in the mirror, you'll give yourself a good laugh and you'll remember not to take everything so seriously.

2.　Make a cup of soothing herbal tea, light a fragrant candle, and sit and sip quietly. Empty your mind and focus on the flame for a mini-meditation session.

3.　If you have a cat or dog, take five minutes to pet him/her. If your pet is too energetic to sit quietly, spend five minutes playing together instead. It's sure to cheer you both up.

4.　Take a bubble bath. Or fill the tub partway with warm water and scented bath oil, then sit on the edge and soak your feet.

5.　Go for a walk, preferably in a park or another scenic locale. If you're at work, head out for a brisk stroll around the block. Even five minutes of stretching and moving can do wonders to calm your nerves.

6.　Close your eyes; visualize yourself in a calm, restorative setting (walking along a wooded path, sitting in a garden); and take ten deep, slow breaths.

7.　Call a friend who cheers you up and talk about a happy or humorous subject—reminisce about the great vacation you took together, compare notes on your all-time worst dates—whatever will take your mind off your responsibilities. Make sure she's not too busy to chat first, and *don't* bring up the wedding.

8. Tackle a small non-wedding-related task you can complete quickly. Clean the fridge, sort through mail or magazines, or paint your fingernails (it's a great way to keep yourself from munching on junk food). If you're feeling overwhelmed, finish *anything* that will give you a sense of accomplishment and, hence, control.

The Date Dilemma

For bridesmaids who are not married or involved in a serious relationship, the issue of whether to bring a date often poses a dilemma. First, make sure you're allowed to bring someone (if your invitation does not say "and guest," the decision has been made for you). If you have been invited to bring a guest, ask yourself the following questions.

1. How will your potential date feel about the fact that you'll be unavailable for a good part of the time leading up to and during the wedding? Does he know other guests? Will he be comfortable on his own?

2. How will you feel being away from him? Will you be so distracted by his presence or worried about him being bored that you won't be able to devote your full attention to the bride when she needs you most?

3. How does he handle himself in social settings? Is he gregarious and good at small talk? Is he shy and introverted?

4. If dancing will be a big part of the reception, how does he feel about it? If he suffers from deer-in-the-headlights syndrome the moment the music starts up, you may find yourself looking longingly at other male guests...

5. If you'll be seated at a head table with only members of the wedding party, will you really get to spend enough time together to make it worth his while?

6. Is he the jealous type, likely to balk at every old acquaintance you chat with? Will any old flames be among the guests? If so, could this cause problems?

7. Are the other bridesmaids bringing dates?

8. Is the wedding local, or will you need to travel? If the latter, what will the sleeping arrangements be? Going on a trip like this may be too complicated if the guy under consideration is a casual date. But if you've found a new love, the event could provide the perfect excuse to take a mini-vacation—just tack on a few days afterward.

9. Is the idea of attending a wedding together likely to bring up difficult issues in your own relationship? If you've been hankering for a ring for the past two years and he's been stalling (or vice versa), bringing him to your friend's wedding could aggravate the situation and elevate your stress level. Plus, wedding guests have been known to speculate—even ask outright—whether a promising-looking couple will be the ones headed to the altar next.

REFLECTIONS FROM REAL BRIDESMAIDS

"When I was my best friend's maid of honor, my boyfriend actually volunteered to fly to my hometown with me and be my date for the wedding. He hung out with my parents while I fulfilled all those last-minute maid-of-honor duties, and he made small talk with my old high school friends during the cocktail hour while I posed for bridal party portraits. I couldn't believe how patient and good-natured he was through it all. It's one of the things that made me realize what a great guy he was. Four years later we got married, and my best friend paid us back by being my honor attendant while her husband played the patient date waiting in the wings.**"**

—ANNE MONROE

Chapter Three

Wedding Party Politics

How to Become a Master Diplomat Overnight

Expert negotiator. Crisis manager. Problem solver. Creative strategist. Goodwill ambassador. The skills you're likely to develop as a bridesmaid could make you a viable candidate for a job at the United Nations. Finding a way to work harmoniously with the other people involved in the wedding can be among your biggest challenges. Egos, opinions, and spending limits often clash. The good news is that you can resolve any conflict as long as you remember that you all love the bride and share the common goal of wanting her to be happy.

Challenging Personalities and How to Deal with Them

The dictator: This bossy bridesmaid (or mother of the bride) steamrolls over everyone else and rejects creative input. She's likely to plan the whole shower without consulting anyone, single-handedly select a group gift, and start ordering the other bridesmaids around like an army sergeant dealing with new recruits.

How to handle her: Resist the urge to be defensive or accusatory. In her mind she's just being efficient; she doesn't necessarily mean to imply that you're all inept. Listen to her without interrupting, then offer your own input in a nonthreatening way. It helps to paraphrase what she's said (a tactic that shows you understand and acknowledge her ideas) and make her think that she's helped you come up with your suggestions. Example: "Your idea of a linen shower for Jane sounds great. I was just thinking that Jane often talks about what fun you two had in the Bahamas last spring. She *lives* for the beach. Do you think she might like it if we included beach towels and other beach-related items in the shower gifts?"

The compulsive competitor: She seems convinced that you're all locked in a battle for the bride's affection. She repeatedly insists or insinuates that she's closer to the bride than anyone else and, therefore, knows best.

How to handle her: Don't get sucked into the rivalry. Realize that insecurity is motivating her behavior. Reassure her if you're confident enough. Example: "Sue's going to love the bridal trivia game you created for her; it's such a special gesture and really shows how well you know her." Remember, this isn't a reality TV show—no one is getting eliminated. The bride loves you all; that's why she chose you as bridesmaids.

The chronic procrastinator: This indecisive bridesmaid drives everyone crazy with her stonewalling. On the surface she seems enthusiastic and eager to please, but all of her well-intentioned promises fall through. At the last minute, you discover that she never ordered the cake for the shower, never made that handcrafted scrapbook for the bride, or never called the nail salon to find out whether it could be reserved for a private party.

How to handle her: Be aware that she means well. Her stalling most likely stems from a fear of letting anyone down. Secretly she suspects that the bakery won't agree to whip up a one-of-a-kind butterscotch-and-chocolate cake decorated in the bride's wedding colors, thinks any scrapbook she designs will fall short of expectations, or fears that booking private manicures is beyond her budget. But she's too polite or shy to disappoint everyone by pointing out her concerns. When you realize she's dragging her feet, try to clarify the issue and help her articulate what she's worried about. Listen for hints; she's probably trying to express the problem subtly. Help her solve it, or give her an easy out. Example: "Booking a nail salon would be a big expense. I'll bet Kris would be just as happy if we took her out for brunch instead. What do you think?" Reassure her after a decision has been made, as she'll probably still be plagued with guilt and self-doubt.

The constant complainer: The shower's impossible to plan, the dress makes her look fat, and she can't believe the bride chose *that* song for the wedding party's dance. This bridesmaid's litany of laments seems endless. The implication is that she's been wronged and everyone else should be trying to fix the situation.

How to handle her: One of two impulses is probably driving her perpetual grumbling. The first possibility is that she feels guilty about something. Perhaps she's too busy to put much effort into planning the prewedding parties, or maybe she suspects that the unflattering dresses were chosen to accommodate her own figure flaws. Whatever reason lies behind her guilt, she believes on some level that complaining about problems beyond her control will shift the blame or keep people from noticing her own shortcomings. The second possibility is that she feels powerless about decisions that affect her, and this is the only way she can assert herself. Listen patiently, but don't agree or apologize. Ask problem-solving questions: "What games do *you* think we should play at the shower?" Brainstorm with her on concrete solutions: "I know an affordable seamstress who could do a few more alterations on the dress for you. Here's her number." Don't get drawn into her negativity or her habit of accusing others. Above all, don't lose your cool and blurt out, "If you'd just stop complaining and pitch in..."

The yes-woman: Almost annoyingly agreeable, she seems to concur with everything you suggest. But then she either doesn't deliver on what she promised or you hear through the grapevine that she's been bad-mouthing your ideas to the other bridesmaids.

How to handle her: She really, really wants to be liked—so much so that she's afraid to say no to you, even if she knows she doesn't have time to decorate the shower invitations by hand or thinks kidnapping the bride for a surprise ski weekend is a lousy idea. If she shares her true feelings with one other bridesmaid who relays the comments to you, it's probably because that bridesmaid is the only person with whom she feels she can be truthful without risking disapproval or rejection. Don't be confrontational or accuse her of passive-aggressive behavior. Ask straightforward, nonthreatening questions, and encourage her to be honest about her opinions. Reassure her that no one will think less of her: "I know creating the invitations is a huge job, requiring a lot of time and effort. Do you think it would be more realistic to go through a stationer?" Try to keep her from making promises she can't keep, and give her a way to say no.

Common Challenges and How to Solve Them

Long-distance logistics: If you live in a different city from the bride and other bridesmaids, you may not be able to attend all of the prewedding events. Tell the others up front how much travel your budget allows for and how many parties you expect to make. Offer to assist in whatever way you can with the planning or to take on more responsibilities during the wedding weekend to make up for what you will have missed in the months leading up to the big day. You might be asked to chip in for the shower and bachelorette party even if you're not attending; you're not obligated to do so, but if you can afford it, it's a nice gesture and will certainly put you in a favorable light with the rest of the crew. You can either send a set amount or pay for a specific element, such as the bridal shower flowers or a few bottles of bubbly for the bachelorette bash.

Feeling like the odd girl out: All of the other bridesmaids have known one another forever or seem to be bonding effortlessly while you remain alone on the outskirts. Don't stress about it. Be gracious, friendly, and cheerful, and remember that this isn't a popularity contest. Concentrate on your friend the bride. Your only goal is to send her into wedded life in style, not to build lasting relationships with her former college roommates. One of the worst things bridesmaids can do is lose sight of their mission and develop cliques within the party. So if you're hitting it off divinely with your friend's friends but notice another bridesmaid feeling left out, do your best to bring her into the fold.

Bridesmen: If you're in a mixed-gender group of attendants, make no assumptions about the prewedding parties. Get everyone together as soon as possible and come up with a game plan. Be aware that if you plan a traditional shower and bachelorette party, the guy(s) may opt out, leaving you saddled with the bulk of the work—and the bill. Often when a bride includes attendants of both sexes, the groom does the same. This might be the type of couple who'd love a coed shower (see page 89) and a joint bachelor-bachelorette party. (Bonus: You can include the groom's attendants, too, which means more hands on deck to help and more people to split the tab.) The dynamics will be a bit different with men in the picture, but the etiquette rules for encouraging and respecting the opinions of the *entire* bridal party still apply. Do your best to make male bridal attendants feel included.

Bickering bridesmaids: Unfortunately, weddings can bring out the petty, selfish sides of some people. Feuding bridesmaids will make everyone in the party miserable and bring the poor bride to tears long before she says "I do." If any of the women in the party are openly hostile or sniping behind each other's backs, encourage them to talk it out. Don't take sides, even if you feel that someone is in the wrong. Remind them that they owe it to the bride to get along for the next few months. If you're one of the people involved, take the high road and resolve to end the dispute. Invite the other woman (or women) to lunch and try to establish a truce.

Large wedding parties: Being one of a dozen bridesmaids has decided advantages. There are plenty of helping hands to go around. And many shoulders to cry on means a stressed-out bride will always find someone with ample spare time and sympathy. What's more, with all of those people contributing to the group expenses, you might really be able to throw the shower of the century without going broke. On the downside, there are many more opinions and ideas to contend with, and the potential for misunderstandings and clashes increases exponentially. To make things run smoothly, it's crucial to set up clear channels of communication early on and to appoint a single leader (usually the maid of honor).

Small wedding parties: Working with only one or two other attendants can be a true bonding experience. Chances are you'll get to know one another extremely well by the time the wedding arrives. You might even exchange tearful good-byes when it's all over or keep in touch for years to come. On the flip side, the experience can be a long haul if you don't hit it off. You'll have fewer hands on deck, so it's essential for you to share the workload equally, even if that requires some sacrifices on your part. It's also important to set realistic goals about how elaborate the parties will be and how much money you'll spend on them (particularly if you'll need to fly to the wedding or shell out a considerable sum for your attire). Think about enlisting help from some of the bride's other close friends or relatives when it comes to planning the shower or bachelorette party.

Message for the Maid of Honor

1. Make an effort to solicit the other bridesmaids' opinions and include them in major decisions. If possible, get together or arrange a conference call so you can develop a "to do" list for each major project as a group.

2. Whenever possible, let the other members of the bridal party choose their own responsibilities. People tend to be more productive and enthusiastic when they're playing to their strengths and interests.

3. Offer ample encouragement and thanks. It never hurts to send a group e-mail acknowledging a bridesmaid for the efforts she has put forth. Example: "A big round of applause to Amy for compiling that priceless photo collection of Debby's worst fashion faux pas. We can't wait to see the look on Debby's face when she's presented with it at the bachelorette party!"

4. If you see trouble signs (review the Challenging Personalities section on pages 40 to 42 for red flags), work around them. Does one bridesmaid have a penchant for proposing elaborate decorative touches that never materialize? Don't put her in charge of important elements for the prewedding parties; give her only little extras that won't affect the outcome of an event. Is another bridesmaid prone to putting a discouraging spin on everything? Encourage her to communicate with you directly, and don't ask her to pass on wedding-related updates to the rest of the party; you don't want her spreading pessimism to the other bridesmaids.

Chapter Four

The (Dreaded) Dress and Beauty Basics

Butt of countless jokes and bane of many a woman's existence, the bridesmaid dress is still often seen as the strongest disincentive for agreeing to stand up in a friend's wedding. Happily, though, trends are shifting. This means there's a good chance you might end up in a dress you actually like.

The Good News

❋ More and more brides are inviting their attendants to pick out their own dresses or at least giving them some say in what they'll wear at the wedding.

❋ It's now de rigueur for bridesmaids to wear complementary, rather than identical, outfits. Often the way in which this works is that the bride picks a dress designer and color, and the bridesmaids then choose from a selection of silhouettes; this approach enables each woman to pick a style that flatters her figure.

※ Once-taboo colors such as slimming black and understated ivory are gaining popularity in the realm of bridesmaid attire. Neutral shades like these don't clash dramatically with skin tones the way jewel tones and pastels can. Plus, these versatile colors give you a better chance of being able to wear the ensemble for some other occasion.

※ Designers are expanding and updating their lines of bridesmaid dresses, introducing more streamlined, sophisticated silhouettes, as well as two-piece ensembles.

※ Ready-to-wear cocktail dresses, sheaths, and chic suits from department stores, designer outlets, and other nonbridal shops have come into vogue for bridesmaids. This trend, too, contributes to the likelihood of your wearing a simpler, less fussy style.

Finance FAQs

Who pays for the dress and accessories? You do. Like it or not, you are expected to foot the bill for not only your dress, but your entire wedding day wardrobe, including whatever shoes, jewelry, and other accessories the bride decides you should wear. Some very generous brides do spring for part of the dress; others give wraps or earrings as bridesmaid gifts, with the understanding that they'll be worn at the wedding. You can't count on such gestures, though.

What if the dress exceeds my spending limit? Unfortunately, there's not much you can do. Technically, you agreed to pay the tab without blanching when you signed on to be a bridesmaid. If the bride asks for your input when she's shopping, you can gently steer her toward dresses in your price range—or at least toward ready-to-wear styles you'll be able to use again (the latter approach won't save you money, but it's a better investment).

How much should I expect to pay? On average, between $150 and $300 for the dress, though bridesmaids interviewed for this book paid as little as $80 and as much as $500. Alterations can add $50 to $150 or more, depending on whether or not you go through a salon, the geographic area, how complicated the work is, and how much is being done. To be on the safe side, budget another $50 for each of the following: shoes, jewelry, and lingerie (strapless bras, slips, crinolines, etc.). If you're an out-of-town attendant, you may need to factor in the cost of shipping the dress. Last but not least, if you'll be participating in a prewedding hair and makeup session, plan on spending another $50 to $150 (here, too, amounts vary according to geographic region and what you're having done).

Salon Basics

❈ Shops that specialize in bridesmaid attire tend to have only sample sizes for you to try on. Based on your measurements—which will be taken by a sales consultant or which you'll need to provide if you're an out-of-town attendant— a dress in the appropriate size will be ordered for you.

❈ If you don't live in the area and will need to phone in your measurements (bust, waist, hips, and sometimes height), find a professional seamstress or tailor to take them for you. You'll get more accurate numbers than if you attempt to do it yourself. It's a good idea to call the dress salon ahead of time and find out exactly what measurements they need and how they want them taken.

❈ If you'll be wearing a gown from a bridal designer, be prepared to jump up a size or two. Like wedding gowns, bridesmaid dresses tend to run small because they're based on standard measurements from the 1940s. Note, too, that your dress size will be based on your *largest* measurement, since it's easier to take in or shorten a garment than it is to let one out. If you're curious about your size, ask to see the shop's dress charts.

※ When you order a dress from a bridal salon, you'll probably be asked to pay a deposit and sign a contract. Such contracts typically include, but are not necessarily limited to, the following: the name of the designer or manufacturer, the style number, the color, the fabric, the size, any special modifications to the dress (such as substituting covered buttons for standard ones), and all fees (including the deposit amount and due date and the balance amount and due date). Dress contracts also usually include the shop's cancellation policy.

※ It takes most salons specializing in bridesmaid dresses three months or more to get a dress into the store after it's been ordered (some require as much as six months); some stores will fulfill the order in less time for a rush fee. Once the garment is in, it will most likely need to be altered; usually getting a dress to look its best involves two fittings. Ideally, the dress should arrive in the store two months before the wedding so that you have time for adjustments.

※ Note that not all stores selling bridesmaid attire do alterations.

SIZING UP THE SITUATION

IF YOUR ONLY CHOICE IS TO TAKE YOUR OWN MEASUREMENTS, contact the dress salon about the specifics of how to do so. Typically, your bust measurement is taken around the widest part of your back and the fullest part of your chest (not under the bust line), your waist measurement about an inch above your navel, and your hips at their widest point (to find the right spot for the latter, put your hands on your hips with your thumbs at your waist, and measure around the point where your pinkies touch your body). To determine the right length for a long gown, you typically measure from your shoulder to the floor (you'll probably need a second pair of hands for this one). Measurements are usually taken while you're clothed in just your undergarments (don't wear a heavily padded bra).

Message for the Maid of Honor

❦ The bride may enlist you to act as coordinator for the bridesmaid dresses. As point person, your duties will probably entail the following:

1. Providing the bridesmaids with all of the information they need, such as the name of the store where the dresses are being purchased, the name and contact information for the sales associate handling the order, when the bridesmaids need to be measured at the salon or the date by which they need to send in their measurements, and when the contracts and deposits are due

2. Following up with the bridesmaids and the store to make sure that everyone has done what they're supposed to (measurements are in, signed contracts have been returned, deposits have been paid, and the order has been placed)

3. Making sure that each bridesmaid has a swatch of the dress, if everyone is getting shoes dyed to match

4. Coordinating the bridesmaids' fittings after the dresses have arrived

5. Arranging for the dresses to be picked up

❦ The bride might also put you in charge of picking out accessories, such as shoes and wraps to coordinate with the bridesmaid dresses.

❦ Note that some brides call attention to the maid of honor's special status by having her wear a different dress than the rest of the bridal party, especially if the group is large.

☜ If the bride is letting you choose your own attire, follow the guidelines starting on page 54 to make sure it suits the wedding's level of formality and the bride's vision. It's also a good idea to find out what colors the mothers of the bride and groom plan to wear so that you can avoid those hues.

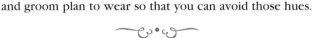

General Shopping Tips

1. Style your hair and put on your makeup before you head out to shop. You'll feel better in everything you try on, and you'll generally get better service.

2. Buy your shoes and any special lingerie needed in time for your first fitting to ensure the best alterations. If you can't get the shoes by this point, bring heels of the same height as those you intend to wear to the wedding.

3. Check whether you'll need a slip to keep the skirt of your dress from becoming transparent when backlit.

4. Consider minor alterations even for ready-to-wear in your normal size. A great fit makes any dress look better and makes you feel better wearing it.

5. Ask the salon or dress shop staff for advice about the best way to store the dress to protect it from wrinkling before the wedding, as well as the best way to get rid of any wrinkles should some appear.

6. Ask the sales associate what to do in case of minor stains and, if you hope to wear the dress again, whether there are any special cleaning instructions.

Following Orders: When the Bride Selects the Dress

※ If she asks for your input, give it. If she invites you to shop for bridesmaid dresses with her, make the time, no matter how busy your schedule is. Not only is this part of your job as a bridesmaid, but participating in this way gives you a better chance of ending up with something flattering for the wedding. Be tactful but honest with your opinions, and if you are familiar with the other bridesmaids, consider how the options will look on them (wouldn't you want them to do the same for you?).

※ If the dresses are being ordered, take note of the payment terms—specifically what type of payment is accepted, the deposit amount and due date, and the balance amount and due date. Some brides pass on this kind of information themselves, others designate the maid of honor to act as point person, and still others may ask that you be in contact with the store itself.

※ Pay up promptly. You don't want the whole bridal party's order to be delayed and the dresses to be late because you dropped the ball, nor do you want to be responsible for everyone getting slapped with a rush fee.

※ Likewise, provide your measurements or make yourself available to be measured at the salon within the designated time frame. Do not make the bride or maid of honor chase after you. They have enough on their plates.

※ Find out if alterations are included in the price of the dress; if they're extra, contact the sales associate to find out what the cost will be (often, you'll be given only an estimate). If the fee seems excessive, consider hiring your own seamstress. You might be able to get someone to alter all of the bridesmaid gowns more affordably.

※ If you live in a different city from the bride and will need to have your dress shipped, ask the sales associate about the cost.

※ If you're having the dress shipped to you, find out when the shop can guarantee it will arrive. You'll want to receive it with enough time to take it to a local seamstress or tailor for adjustments if it doesn't fit correctly. To give yourself a decent cushion, aim to have the dress in your hands six weeks in advance of the wedding. If you're cutting it close, line up a seamstress ahead of time.

※ If you'll be arriving in town and picking up your dress just before the wedding (not the ideal approach), find out whether a seamstress at the salon will be available for last-minute snips and tucks. If not, line up a tailor in the area ahead of time (one of the local bridesmaids might be able to help you find someone).

※ Resist the urge to complain about the dress to the other bridesmaids or anyone else who knows the bride or groom. It's amazing how often little digs get over-heard, passed around, and routed back to the very person who's not supposed to hear them.

※ Refrain from catty comments about how the other bridesmaids' figures or figure flaws are dictating the dress styles—regardless of whether they're petite, perky size twos or Amazons who need uniforms built for a linebacker. The same holds true if each attendant is allowed to select her own dress: Don't snipe about the other women's choices.

Choosing Your Own Dress

※ Have a talk with the bride to get a sense of how involved she wants to be in the selection of dresses. Does she want you to run all the details by her, or is she so swamped with other aspects of the wedding that she'll be relieved to have one less item on her checklist? Would she prefer to see a few of your favorites and approve them before you make a purchase? Take your cues from her. If she wants to be less involved, have a brief chat with her to cover the basics. Following are some key questions to ask.

1. How formal does she want the dress to be?

2. Does she want the bridesmaids to wear identical dresses or sport a variety of looks?

3. Does she have a color preference—or any colors that she wants you to avoid?

4. Are there any styles or looks she wants you to stay away from (e.g., miniskirts, two-piece ensembles, prints)?

5. Does she want all of the dresses to be the same length, and if so, where should the hemline fall?

6. If the ceremony is a religious one, does the house of worship have any restrictions regarding attire (e.g., covered shoulders, no open-toe shoes, etc.)?

7. What does the bride's dress look like? (If she's wearing a simple modern sheath, you'll want to avoid elaborate brocades and corseting.)

※ Glance through bridal magazines to get a feel for styles and designers you like. You can also check out the latest collections of bridesmaid-gown designers on their websites—an especially convenient approach if you and the bride live in different cities and you want to review possibilities with her. (For a list of websites, see page 145.)

※ Compare notes with the other women in the wedding party. If the bride wants you in different outfits, make sure you don't end up wearing the same thing as someone else. Ideally, the various ensembles should have some unity in terms of formality, seasonality, and style (it creates a more cohesive, elegant look in the photographs and at the ceremony). If you haven't been given guidelines, ask the other bridesmaids what length of hem they're wearing, what type of sleeve, and what fabric. If everyone else is opting for tea-length dresses with short sleeves, do you really want to be the lone bridesmaid in a strapless number with a skirt that barely brushes your knees?

※ Steer clear of anything too loud or too sexy. Your dress shouldn't draw attention from the bride. Besides, as a bridesmaid you're likely to get more than enough unwanted attention from male guests who have downed a few cocktails.

※ Avoid anything that looks good only if you hold your stomach in or don't eat for hours before wearing it; you'll want to feel comfortable, not fret over every morsel that touches your lips. Never buy a dress expecting to lose weight or get in shape in order for it to fit.

※ Once you've located the dress you want, put it on hold, and ask the bride if she wants to come with you to see it before you make your purchase. If she lives too far away for an in-person look, you can send or e-mail her a photograph of the garment.

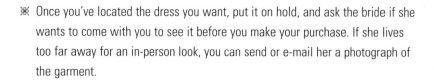

ALTERNATE APPROACH

IT MAY SEEM AS THOUGH FINDING A DRESS YOU LIKE is as difficult as finding the right guy. If you're having trouble with the former (you'll need a different book for the latter), consider hiring a dressmaker to make one for you; just be sure that the person you hire is a pro, and allot plenty of time for multiple alterations.

Money-Saving Tips

※ Start shopping early to take advantage of sales and to give yourself plenty of time to look. A last-minute quest for a dress is a sure way to overpay.

※ Don't limit your search to salons specializing in bridesmaid attire. Check out department stores, dress shops, and outlet malls.

※ To avoid the cost of alterations, consider a two-piece ensemble or separates that allow you to buy a top and bottom in different sizes for a better fit (just make sure that the bride doesn't object to this look).

※ Restrict yourself to styles that don't require a special bra. This tactic not only spares you from springing for special lingerie, it saves you time trying to find a bra that works with the outfit.

※ Consider borrowing a dress from a friend.

※ Look for simple styles that don't include beading or lacework, as these details tend to jack up the price. Likewise, less formal dresses usually don't cost as much as formal gowns.

Salon Strategies for Shopping Solo

If you're selecting your own dress but still plan on going through a shop that specializes in bridesmaid attire, see Salon Basics on page 49 and keep the following points in mind.

✳ Start the hunt as early as possible, since many salons carrying bridesmaid attire will charge you a rush fee if you order past a certain point. As noted earlier, it can take three to six months for a salon to fulfill orders, and you need to leave time for alterations after the dress arrives. That said, your time frame will obviously depend on the bride's. If she's putting the whole wedding together in only six months, you may not be able to choose a dress until two or three months before the big day. If a salon can't work with the time frame you've been given, try another one or consider purchasing off the rack.

✳ Call before heading to a salon, as many require appointments.

✳ If your schedule permits, try to make an appointment during the week, as these stores tend to be crowded on the weekends.

✳ Find out how long it takes for the dress to come in to the shop and how long alterations take; if you'll be taking the garment to an outside tailor for adjustments, look into how long that person needs. If possible, arrange to have the dress hit the store two months before the wedding to allow for alterations and unforeseen delays.

✳ Ask for a fabric swatch or two; the bride might want one when she's picking out bouquets, and you'll need one if you're having shoes dyed to match.

✳ Do not wait until the day before you're departing for the wedding to pick up your altered dress, as you'll be in trouble if the adjustments were not done correctly.

Style Points for the Pregnant Attendant

Once taboo, serving as a bridesmaid when you're expecting is now perfectly acceptable. The biggest challenge is anticipating your measurements. Below are a few pointers.

※ If it's not your first pregnancy, don't rely on experience as a gauge; just because you didn't "pop" until the sixth month last time doesn't guarantee you'll be able to squeeze into a size eight at the same point this time around.

※ Many designers of bridesmaid dresses can alter their styles to accommodate pregnant tummies, but your best bet is to ask the bride whether she's willing to let you wear a stylish maternity dress in a color that matches or complements the outfits of the other bridesmaids. Maternity shops and catalogs stock a variety of dressy designs in styles that are flattering for moms-to-be, including ones with an Empire waist and A-line numbers made of swingy, stretchy fabrics.

※ If you love tight-fitting, belly-accenting maternity wear, find out what the bride thinks of this style before buying; she might prefer a more understated look. The last thing either of you wants is every eye on your abdomen as the couple exchanges vows.

※ This is the one time you *should* wait as long as possible to purchase your shoes. Why? Moms-to-be often go up a shoe size as the due date nears.

WARDING OFF WRINKLES

A S SOON AS YOU GET THE DRESS HOME, hang it in your closet so that there's plenty of space on either side of it. Squeezing it in too tightly between other clothes can bring on the wrinkles. Obviously, you want the dress to look its best on the big day.

The Lingo

When shopping for bridesmaid dresses and/or discussing various attire options with the bride and other attendants, you'll be confronted with a whole slew of terms that you probably don't come across in everyday conversation. To help you understand what may seem like a foreign language, here are some basic terms and definitions.

Silhouettes

A-line/princess: A popular choice because it flatters most figures, this design has a slightly tapered waist, from which the skirt flows gently outward, replicating the shape of a capital letter A.

Ball gown: This style has a dropped waist and a full, rounded, floor-length skirt. This is not a common silhouette for bridesmaid dresses, though the bride might be decked out in this type of dress.

Empire: Offering a romantic, period look (think *Pride and Prejudice*), this design features a high waistline that hits right under the bust and a straight or A-line skirt. It hides a thick waist and flatters most body types, though those with an hourglass figure are better off avoiding this style. The silhouette works well for pregnant bridesmaids and gives the illusion of height to petite women.

Sheath: Creating a modern look, this style is straight and slim, often featuring indentations (darts or seams) at the waist. Sheaths tend to suit slender women with relatively narrow hips, and are less desirable for those with a full figure or short waist.

Slip dress: Body-hugging and cut on the bias, this style usually comes in clingy, satiny fabrics and looks best on slim women.

Skirt Lengths

Knee-length: The skirt just covers the knee.

Tea-length: The hem hits at the center of the calf.

Ballerina-/ankle-length: The hem falls either just above or at the ankle.

Floor-length: The hem skims the floor.

Necklines

Cowl: This neckline contains extra fabric that hangs in draped folds.

Halter: Fabric loops around the back of the neck, leaving the shoulders, and often the back, bare. The neckline itself can be high or low.

Jewel: Like a T-shirt collar, this rounded neckline rests at the base of the throat.

Off-the-shoulder: This revealing neckline rests just below the shoulders, where it merges with the sleeves. The style shows off a woman's collarbone and shoulders.

Portrait: A variation of the off-the-shoulder cut, it offers a bit more coverage around the neckline.

Sabrina/bateau: This demure design follows the curves of the collarbone, cutting straight across the body from the tip of one shoulder to the other. The front and back are mirror images.

Scoop: In the front, this neckline dips to form a U or a square shape. The back either mirrors the front or simply cuts straight across.

Sweetheart: This cleavage-enhancing design mimics the top half of a heart.

V-Neck: The front of this neckline creates a V-shape.

Sleeves

Bell: This sleeve is fitted from the shoulder to just short of the elbow, where it starts to flare outward as it descends toward the wrist.

Cap: Short and fitted or slightly puffed, this sleeve conceals just the top of the shoulder.

Three-quarter length: This sleeve extends to the midpoint between the elbow and wrist.

T-shirt: Like the name suggests, this design is short and simple, bearing the same basic lines as the sleeve found on a T-shirt.

The Lowdown on Lingerie

It's not uncommon for bridesmaid dresses to require special bras that are strapless or have low backs. If you're not sure what type would work best with your dress, ask the sales staff. Or, if you're not ordering through a salon, take the dress to a lingerie shop for advice and try it on with the different styles suggested. (If this is your first time being professionally fitted for a bra, don't be surprised to hear that you've been wearing the wrong size all these years.) For tight-fitting dresses, you may want to consider control-top hose, seamless undies, or a thong to avoid the dreaded VPL (visible panty line), as well as a slightly padded, smooth satin bra. For full skirts, you may need a crinoline or petticoat for extra flounce. Here are a few common bra terms.

Balcony bra: Also called a balconette, shelf, or demi-cup bra, this undergarment features wide-set straps and cups that do not come up as high on your bust as a traditional bra (thus, it can be a good choice to wear with a low-cut dress). Usually, it provides a push-up effect.

Plunge bra: The cups are cut on the diagonal with a very low center so that the bra doesn't peek out from a dress with a plunging neckline; this bra is often designed to enhance cleavage.

Racerback bra: The straps taper inward as they descend from the shoulder down the back, merging into one connected piece.

Convertible bra: Usually an underwire variety, this versatile bra has straps that can be rearranged to achieve a cross-back, halter, or single-strap configuration; they can also be removed altogether.

Bustier: Also referred to as a longline bra, this strapless piece of lingerie has an underwire construction and extends to the waist, fitting snugly around the body. It tends to stay in place better than a regular strapless bra, especially if you're full-figured. What's more, it can help to cinch your waist and flatten your stomach; beware, though, that it can also make your hips bulge below the point where the undergarment ends.

Shoes, Wraps, and Accessories

※ If you're buying your own accessories, shop for items that are in keeping with the wedding's level of formality, time of day, and season, as well as the style of your dress.

※ Forgo gloves unless everyone else is wearing them. Short gloves are paired with short or long sleeves. Over-the-elbow gloves are worn with sleeveless or strapless dresses and are usually reserved for highly formal events.

※ If you're wearing a strapless dress but the ceremony site requires that your shoulders be covered, you'll need a short jacket, shawl, or some other pretty wrap. You'll probably need one anyway if the site is air-conditioned or if it's an outdoor evening wedding during a time of year when the weather gets a bit chilly after the sun goes down.

※ If you're having shoes dyed to match the dress, be sure to provide a swatch to the professional performing this service.

* If you're choosing your own shoes for a wedding during which you'll be spending time outdoors and walking on grass, avoid satin, silk, or other materials you can't easily wipe clean. Opt for smooth leather if possible.

* So that you're comfortable on your feet—whether standing during a long ceremony or dancing the night away—break in your shoes before the wedding day. Simply wear them a few times around the house, where they won't get dirty. You'll want to scuff the bottoms as well to avoid slipping. If the shoes have slippery soles, you might also opt to buy inexpensive stick-on no-slip grips at a drugstore or shoe store.

* Find out if the bride wants you to wear jewelry and if she has any specific requests. If she's leaving the choice to you, opt for an understated look. Hopefully, you already own something that will work so you can save some money in this area. If you're traveling, you may want to avoid bringing precious pieces or ones with sentimental value so that you don't have to worry about leaving them in the hotel room or the hotel safe.

* You'll need a small evening bag, just big enough for a few cosmetics and essentials. Finding a safe place to stash it can be a challenge. If you're bringing a date, have him hold it (it should be diminutive enough to be tucked into his jacket pocket or slipped unobtrusively under his ceremony program). If there's a bridal suite, you might be able to leave it there. You'll need both hands for your bouquet during the ceremony, for greeting guests at the cocktail hour, and for hitting the dance floor at the reception, so don't put anything so valuable in your purse that you'll feel compelled to check on it every ten minutes.

How to Feel Fabulous—
No Matter What You're Wearing

1. If you'll be permitted to do your own makeup at the wedding, splurge on fancy new lipstick, blush, and/or eye shadow. Test out the products several times far in advance to make sure you don't have an allergic reaction.

2. Bring your favorite perfume and skin lotion. So what if you can't control your hair or makeup? You can make sure your skin feels silky and you smell divine. Caveat: If it's an outdoor wedding, you may want to forgo this treat so as not to give bees or mosquitoes any added incentive.

3. Indulge in luxurious new nylons and panties. At least you'll feel great *underneath* your clothes.

4. Go to bed early the night before the wedding. A good night's sleep will do wonders for both your look and your outlook.

5. Purchase a pair of gel pads to slip inside your shoes. They'll add a spring to your step and keep your feet from aching at the altar or on the dance floor.

6. Smile and stand up straight. It's the same old advice you probably got from your mom as a kid, but it's worth following. With good posture, poise, and an air of confidence, you can carry off any dress.

7. Bring a fantastic outfit for the rehearsal dinner and the other events surrounding the wedding. That way the guests—and any interesting men you meet if you're single—will have ample opportunity to see how beautiful you look when you get to pick out your own clothes and style your own hair.

8. Keep it all in perspective. As with other challenges you encounter as a bridesmaid, focus on your friendship with the bride. Is there one memory that crystallizes it? One wonderful gesture she made for you in the past? The more specific the memory, the better. Fixate on it every time you catch sight of your image in the mirror. Remind yourself that the bride is a cherished friend, the kind for whom you'll willingly walk into a room full of people while looking like a giant eggplant. And remember that it's only a few hours out of your life.

Wedding Day Beauty

※ Some brides arrange for the bridesmaids to have their hair and makeup done by a professional. In some cases, the crew heads to a salon; in others, stylists come to the bride's home or the bridal suite at the ceremony site. Be prepared to pay for these services, unless you've been told otherwise.

※ The bride may ask you whether you wish to have your hair and/or makeup done professionally; while an hour or two of beauty with the girls can be great fun, if you're tight on money, you can politely decline.

※ As mentioned in chapter one, if you tend to have allergic reactions to cosmetics, talk to the makeup artist ahead of time about your concerns; inquire as to whether he/she has hypoallergenic products or if you can bring your own.

※ Wear a button-down shirt to any hair or makeup appointment so that when it's time to change, you don't need to pull a shirt over your head.

※ Unless the bride has scheduled manicures for the wedding party, get your nails done a day or two before the wedding. And, unless otherwise instructed, go with clear polish or a French manicure. If you're wearing open-toe shoes, you'll need a pedicure, too.

Things to Do Checklist

The following is a general, comprehensive list of things to do with regard to attire, hair, and makeup. Use it to help you stay on track. Depending on the source of your dress and how involved the bride is, some of these steps may not be relevant to you.

❑ Shop for bridesmaid dresses with bride and/or fellow attendants

❑ Obtain specific guidelines for attire from bride, if she's left the selection up to you (see page 54)

❑ Make final dress selection

❑ Have your measurements taken at the salon, or give these stats, along with your contact information, to the appropriate person

- ❑ Sign and return contract to salon
- ❑ Pay deposit for dress
- ❑ Find out when you'll need to return for fittings
- ❑ Arrange for dress to be shipped, if you aren't local
- ❑ Obtain shoes and lingerie to be worn with dress (in time to bring to first fitting)
- ❑ Have first dress fitting (whether you're going through a salon or taking to a seamstress)
- ❑ Obtain wrap to go with dress, if applicable
- ❑ Figure out what jewelry you'll wear and what evening bag you'll carry; purchase items as needed
- ❑ Have second dress fitting
- ❑ Pick up dress (try on before leaving shop)
- ❑ Pay balance due on dress
- ❑ Take shoes to be dyed to match dress, if applicable
- ❑ Pick up shoes that you had dyed
- ❑ Begin wearing shoes indoors to break them in
- ❑ Make appointment for manicure (and pedicure if wearing open-toe shoes), unless bride has arranged for this
- ❑ Decide how you'll wear your hair, if bride has not given you specific instructions or arranged for a wedding day hair appointment
- ❑ Make sure you have two pairs of nylons in good condition, or purchase new ones
- ❑ Make sure dress is still in good condition (no wrinkles or stray threads)
- ❑ Get manicure
- ❑ Check weather report and make provisions for inclement weather—raincoat, umbrella, waterproof bag for dress and shoes
- ❑ Attend prewedding hair and makeup session, if bride has arranged one
- ❑ Other _____
- ❑ Other _____

Chapter Five

Sensational Showers

Although there is no rule set in stone—or in etiquette books—that a bride's attendants must throw her a shower, most treat her to some sort of gift-giving party in honor of her upcoming nuptials. If you think enough of this woman to agree to be her bridesmaid, chances are she is the kind of friend for whom you'll *want* to plan a great party. The event should leave her with not just a bevy of beautiful presents, but fond memories and a sense of how special she is to her friends and family. Luckily, you already hold the key to designing a party she'll love: You know her. You know her likes and dislikes, her hobbies, her history. Ask yourself what type of event she would enjoy, and plan one tailored to her personality. There's no need to break the bank or throw the shower of the century. As long as you plan the party with care, thought, and a glad heart, the bride is bound to appreciate it.

Bridal Shower Basics

Who should throw the shower? Traditionally, the maid of honor handles this responsibility. However, it's acceptable—and often preferable—for the event to be a joint effort by all or some of the bridesmaids. Cohosting reduces the cost burden and increases the amount of creative energy. If the maid of honor is unable or unwilling to host, another bridesmaid is free to take charge and serve as the point person, with one exception: Showers should not be thrown by the bride's relatives, as this situation can be interpreted as a blatant plea for presents. If all of the bridesmaids are relatives, find a close friend of the bride who is willing to be the nominal host (her name will go on the invitation) and handle the RSVPs; meanwhile, the bridesmaids will actually organize the party behind the scenes and, of course, foot the bill.

When should the shower take place? Anywhere from two months to two weeks before the wedding, preferably between six and three weeks prior. The most important factor when setting the date is to make sure that it works well for the bride. If you plan to surprise her, check with her fiancé and/or her mother to avoid schedule conflicts and enlist their help in ensuring that the bride keeps her calendar clear. If it's impossible to settle on a shower date that allows all of the bridesmaids to attend, choose the one that works best for the bride and the primary host(s)—the one(s) doing the bulk of the work.

How long should the party last? As anyone who has suffered through a four-hour gift-opening marathon knows, showers are far more enjoyable when they don't go on ad infinitum. Establish a specific time frame; try not to let the party run more than three hours. Discuss the time frame with the manager of the venue or the owner of the home where you'll be holding the event. If the shower will be at someone's abode, give yourself plenty of time—ideally, more than you think you'll need since things usually take longer than expected—to set up. It's better to end up with a few spare minutes to catch your breath than to be frantically rushing around as guests start to trickle in. And plan to spend about an hour after the party cleaning up. If you'll be holding the event at a restaurant or another locale with wait staff, arrive well enough in advance to make sure that everything is set up the way you want it and to add any finishing touches of your own (place cards, flowers, decorations for the bride's chair, etc.); you'll also want to be there to greet any guests who arrive early.

Who should pay? Whoever hosts the shower. If no one is willing to help you actually organize the event, you can still ask the other bridesmaids who plan to attend the party to cohost in a financial way; they can either each chip in a set amount or purchase a specific item for the shower. If costs will be split, discuss the budget up front to ensure that it doesn't wildly exceed anyone's finances. If your resources are more restricted than those of your cohosts, be honest about your spending limit and stick to it. You can offer to take on additional responsibilities to compensate for making a smaller financial contribution, though you're not obligated to do so. Don't overextend yourself just to please the other hosts; you'll end up resenting them—and probably the bride—by the time the wedding day arrives.

Do I need to buy a gift if I'm hosting? Yes. Some bridesmaids even decide to buy a group gift in addition to their personal gifts, but it's not a requirement.

The Guest List

How many people should be invited? Some showers are close-knit gatherings of twelve. Others are big, bustling affairs with fifty guests or more. Unless you're lucky enough to have unlimited funds, the number of guests will influence what type of event you hold and where you hold it. For instance, if the guest list is quite large, dinner at the bride's favorite restaurant could be way beyond your budget; you might need to opt for brunch at someone's home.

Who should be invited? Ask the bride—or her fiancé and her mother if you're throwing a surprise shower—for a list of essential names. All bridesmaids and women playing special parts in the ceremony (doing readings, singing solos, etc.) should be invited, as should the mothers, grandmothers, and sisters of the bride and groom. Sisters-in-law and other close relatives and friends are usually included, too; children generally are not. Close pals from work can make the guest list, though coworkers frequently host a separate office shower; try to find out whether the bride's colleagues are planning one for her.

Is it okay to include people who aren't invited to the wedding?
No, unless the wedding will be limited to immediate family or take place in a far-off country. In such cases, most people won't expect to see the couple tie the knot and, thus, shouldn't feel insulted to be invited only to the shower.

What if the bride is having multiple showers? Try to coordinate with the other hosts so that people aren't invited to two events unless they're very close friends or relatives of the bride. If the bride *asks* you to invite someone who is attending another shower, let the guest know that you're asking only for her presence—not a second present.

What if the bride or her mom wants to invite too many people? Be polite but honest about the size of shower you can manage. If you're up for expanding the guest list but lack the funds, ask the bride's mother if she would be willing to pay a set amount while you do the organizing. If she agrees, use your diplomacy skills to prevent her from taking charge. You can offer to include certain elements she wants, though you're not obligated to make major changes. The shower is *your* celebration for the bride—a gift to her from her friends, not her family.

Location, Location, Location

✳ Once you know roughly how many guests to expect and their age range, ask yourself what settings best suit the group.

✳ If you decide to hold the shower in your home or someone else's, make sure it can comfortably accommodate the number of guests you anticipate. If you're expecting upwards of fifteen guests, you should be in a residence that has more than one powder room. Cohosts should arrive early and stay late to help the owner of the home set up and clean up.

✳ If the host has pets, make sure that the bride isn't allergic; you should alert other guests as well.

✳ If you're considering an outdoor event, take into account that you'll need to formulate a feasible backup plan in case of inclement weather. You'll also need to stay away from food that could spoil easily or won't hold up well in the heat. (To make life easier on yourself, you may just want to plan on having an indoor party from the outset.)

Unusual Places and Offbeat Spaces

While restaurants, private clubs, and tearooms are popular spots for showers, an unusual setting can provide a wonderful backdrop or give rise to an imaginative theme. Check with your local chamber of commerce, regional bridal magazines, or party planners for ideas beyond the ordinary. Below are a few twists on the traditional party room.

Landmark building or historic estate: Often rich in charm and atmosphere, these venues make wonderful shower settings, some with catering on-site. If you go this route, make sure your choice isn't too similar to the wedding location.

Boat: Small crafts can be chartered by private parties for short cruises around a harbor or lake, or tables can be reserved on larger dinner cruise boats. Just make sure that the bride doesn't get seasick.

Country house: Ask the bride's friends, family, and fiancé if any of her relatives has a picturesque vacation home not far away and might be willing to offer it as a setting for the party. (Bonus: Holding the event at a relative's house makes it easier to pull off a surprise.)

Booking a Party Space

Following are some pointers for holding a shower at a venue other than someone's personal residence. For a list of questions to ask the manager of a site you're considering, turn to the prepared interview on page 146.

※ Don't book a site without first checking it out in person.

※ If you're considering a restaurant or a place with on-site catering that you're not familiar with, it's a good idea to sample the food before making a decision.

※ Try to book a place where your group will have some privacy. Even if you won't be in a private room, maybe your party can be set up in a secluded corner.

※ Talk to the manager about where exactly your group will be situated. If you've agreed to a certain area within the site, get it in writing.

※ Make sure the setup won't relegate some guests to a table away from the bride and thus leave them feeling left out. If you'd prefer a specific arrangement such as a round table, discuss it with the manager.

※ If you're considering holding the shower at a restaurant, drop by at the same time of day that the party would take place to check out the scene. Is it kiddie hour? Blue-plate-special time? Happy hour? Will the crowd make the atmosphere too chaotic or too staid?

※ Figure out where guests will put gifts. If necessary, ask to have a small gift table set up near the main dining table. This works best in a private room; in the main dining room, you may spend half of your time trying to keep an eye on the presents as strangers pass by en route to the restroom.

※ If the venue will let you use the space for only a certain number of hours, make sure there's enough time that you won't be rushed out the door. If your booking involves a set time frame, let guests know so everyone will arrive promptly. Nothing ruins a party faster than waiters scurrying around snatching coffee cups out of people's hands in their haste to set up for another event. The onus will be on you as the host to keep the party on schedule.

※ Make sure you have your own wait staff, even if the guest list is small. If you'll be signing an agreement, stipulate this in your contract. If a restaurant won't guarantee this, you may want to look elsewhere.

※ If you'll need to settle the bill at the end of the event, be certain the staff knows to discuss billing issues with you discreetly.

Party Supply Central:
To Rent, Buy, or Borrow

If you're planning a large shower in a private home, or if you've chosen a setting where you'll have to bring your own equipment or supplies, you'll need to make a plan for obtaining all the essentials. If you'll be going through a rental company, turn to the prepared interview on page 147 for a list of questions to ask.

❋ If you lack only one serving item—a coffee urn or chafing dish, for instance— try to borrow one.

❋ If you're short on plates or glasses, consider having each cohost bring some. Mismatched stemware and plates in complementary colors can make for a dramatic and eye-catching table. Another alternative is to purchase attractive disposable plates, cups, and tablecloths, which today are available in many elegant and sophisticated designs.

❋ If you'll need quirkier items—helium canisters for balloons, tents and heaters for lavish outdoor events—you'll almost certainly need to rent. Ask around for recommendations.

❋ Before going ahead with any sort of rentals, discuss the costs with your cohosts.

Settling on a Shower Style

What kind of shower should you throw? There are a number of factors to consider when making this decision. Ask yourself the following questions. (For ideas of specific themes, see pages 87 to 90.)

What kind of wedding is the bride planning? The shower's style needn't reflect the wedding's, but you can often find clues to the bride's preferred way of celebrating by analyzing what you know about the big day ahead.

Does she thrive in the spotlight or stick to the sidelines? If she's soft-spoken and easily embarrassed, you can rule out buying racy lingerie and playing risqué games. If she revels in attention, she may delight in such a shower (do take into consideration whether guests from her mother's or grandmothers' generation will appreciate such a theme).

What's her favorite way to spend her free time? If she loves to cook, make food the focal point. Book a table at her favorite restaurant or find out if the place caters, and note a kitchen theme on the invitation so that guests will understand to bring gifts associated with this theme.

What does she need or want in terms of presents? Check her registry to see what she's selected, and determine whether any categories inspire a shower theme.

How did she meet the groom? If they fell in love as grad students studying art history, you might call local galleries to find one with a private room that can be booked for parties, then use famous works of art as the inspiration for invitations and decorations.

Do the bride and groom have any shared hobbies? Their love of wilderness adventures might be the perfect jumping-off point for a "great outdoors" picnic (which could actually be held indoors), with gifts pertaining to camping, hiking, and so on. If you plan an outdoor picnic, be sure to have a backup plan in case of inclement weather.

How does she feel about surprises? Is she the spontaneous type, apt to drop everything and head off for a weekend trip or to invite friends over for dinner on the spur of the moment? If so, chances are she'd thoroughly enjoy a surprise shower. If she's a meticulous planner who's anticipating every detail of the wedding to avoid being taken off guard, she might prefer to know about the party in advance. Keep in mind that if she lives in a different locale and every trip home is tightly booked with wedding-related appointments, a surprise might be too difficult to pull off.

Is this her second marriage? Brides who have been married before are often given showers, though they're usually small and low-key. In such a situation, the bride may not need basic gifts to stock a home. Check the registry, brainstorm with the other bridesmaids, or ask the bride or the groom what types of gifts would be most useful.

What have your experiences been as a guest at other showers? What worked well? What didn't? What made the parties lively, fun, and well paced? What seemed to slow them down? What ideas might you apply to the shower you're planning?

What are your strengths as a hostess? Play to those strengths. If you've no desire to be the next Julia Child, let a caterer or cohost do the cooking while you focus on decorating and devising games to play. If you're a whiz behind the stove but hopeless at organization, turn your energies toward concocting delicious dishes and enlist another bridesmaid to coordinate invitations and RSVPs, or keep the guest list small to minimize the logistical aspects of the planning process.

What is your budget? Plan a party that won't eat up your entire spending allowance for the month. Remember that you'll have other wedding expenses besides this one.

SEMI-SURPRISE

EVEN IF HOLDING A SURPRISE SHOWER IS OUT OF THE QUESTION, you can still veil the event in mystery. Get the bride's input on the date and guest list, but keep all of the other details (menu, theme, favors, etc.) secret. That way, there's still an element of surprise even though the bride knows when the event will be taking place.

How much time can you devote to planning the shower? Don't commit to an event so elaborate or complicated that you'll be a nervous wreck and end up having to call in sick from work for a week to pull it off.

All About Invitations

※ Send written invitations, even for an informal shower. If you spread the word by phone or e-mail, people tend to assume the event is so casual that there's no need to RSVP and you'll need to do a lot of follow-up to determine your head count.

※ Mail the invitations four weeks before the shower, and ask guests to RSVP no later than two weeks before the party itself.

※ Avoid using "Regrets Only" on an invitation, as it makes planning more difficult. There's a good chance you'll waste time and money by making arrangements for more people than actually show up in the end.

※ Designate a single person to handle RSVPs. This will help streamline the process of keeping track of responses.

※ The best way to keep track of responses is to set up a spreadsheet on a home computer. Devote a column to each of the following: invitee's name, mailing address, phone number, e-mail address, response, specific assignment (if applicable). You can also set up a similar chart the old-fashioned way with pencil and paper. At the top of your spreadsheet or chart, be sure to note the date that the invitations were mailed and the date by which invitees were asked to give you their responses.

※ If you're assigning each guest a certain element of a gift-related theme (an hour of the day or a room in the house, for example), you'll need to note for your own reference who has been assigned what and watch for any holes developing as the responses come in (for example, the guests assigned 10:00 P.M., 11:00 P.M., and midnight in an around-the-clock shower have declined). It's a good idea to wait until after you've received the majority of the RSVPs to buy your own gift (ask the other bridesmaids to do the same). That way, you'll be able to fill any gaps as needed.

❋ Put aside a shower invitation for the bride as a keepsake.

Saying It in Style

❋ Shower invitations can be as simple and affordable as the preprinted variety that have blank spaces for filling in all of the details, or you can go the more expensive route and order custom-printed invitations from a stationer. The cost-cutter's approach to personalized invitations is to design them on a home computer and print them on decorative card stock (see the sidebar below).

❋ Consider echoing the shower's theme or locale in the invitation. Or employ the same colors that you're planning to use for the decorations at the event.

❋ To give homemade invitations an air of elegance, place a sheet of vellum on top of the card stock, punch holes through both components, thread ribbon through, and tie in a bow. Make sure that your envelopes can accommodate the greater thickness resulting from this design. And take one assembled invitation—stuffed in its envelope—to the post office to make sure you use the correct amount of postage.

PRACTICAL POINTERS

IF YOU DECIDE TO CREATE THE INVITATIONS ON A HOME COMPUTER, make sure that the material on which you're printing will feed through your printer and not damage it. Look for laser- and inkjet-compatible paper, and consult your user manual for guidelines regarding specialty papers. Also, do a trial run of the invitation on plain paper to make sure that the positioning of the type is correct; that way you won't waste the more expensive material that you're using for the actual invites.

Content

※ Shower invitations should include: the fact that it's a shower; the name of the guest of honor; the date and time; the location; the host's name; RSVP contact information; the date by which to RSVP; and the theme (if there is one). If there are any attire requirements, you'll need to include that information as well. If the party is a surprise, be sure to indicate that key bit of info, too.

※ If you need to assign each guest a specific aspect of the theme (an hour of the day, for instance), you'll need to include this information. If you're having the invitations professionally printed, convey the assignment on a separate piece of paper and slip it into the envelope.

※ If directions to the shower site are complicated, insert a mini-map with a number for guests to call (your cell phone, the restaurant's main number, etc.) in case they get lost.

※ Never include the bride's registry info in an invitation—this is a big faux pas. This information should be communicated only by word of mouth. Make a list of the appropriate stores and the corresponding contact information, and keep a copy next to your phone and one in your purse; that way, when guests inquire— as many undoubtedly will—you'll have the information at your fingertips and you can easily pass it on.

※ If a bride has expressed a preference for cash or gift certificates in lieu of presents, you can politely let guests know that these are acceptable options, but under no circumstances should you say that the bride has asked for them or insist that guests comply, nor should you include this information in the invitation.

The greatest sweetener of human life is friendship.

— Joseph Addison

Planner's Timeline

How much time will it take to pull the shower together? It depends on how elaborate a party you want to throw and how many cohosts there are to pitch in. The bridesmaids interviewed for this book estimated that they devoted an average of two hours a week to planning for two months before the shower, with considerably more the week of the shower. The following checklist should help you budget your time and stay organized. Feel free to expand or compress the time frame and to scrap any steps you don't need.

Three to Four Months Before the Shower
❏ Contact fellow bridesmaids to touch base about the shower, and find out who is willing to cohost; technically this is the maid of honor's responsibility, but if the clock is ticking and there's been no word, another bridesmaid could get in touch with the honor attendant to start the ball rolling
❏ Get an idea of the size of the guest list from the bride or, if the party's a surprise, the groom or the mother of the bride; also discuss what dates will work with the bride's schedule
❏ Brainstorm with cohosts about locations and themes

Two to Three Months Before
❏ Meet/coordinate with cohosts to firm up plans for the type of shower you're planning, and develop a workable budget (see page 85); clarify how costs will be divided
❏ Visit potential venues
❏ Finalize the shower date; clear it with the bride or, if the party will be a surprise, with her fiancé and mother
❏ Book the location, if you're not having the party at someone's home; find out when you need to make your final menu selections (if applicable) and the date by which the venue will need a final head count (the latter is usually a week before the event)

- ❏ Obtain the final guest list from the bride, her mother, or the groom
- ❏ Discuss entertainment, food, and decorations
- ❏ Develop a master list of responsibilities, noting who will handle each; the person in charge should provide all cohosts with a copy of the budget so that everyone stays on track
- ❏ Hire a caterer, if applicable; find out dates for final menu selections and final head count
- ❏ Purchase/create/order invitations
- ❏ Reserve any rental items needed
- ❏ Book any desired entertainment

Two Months Before

- ❏ Obtain phone numbers and addresses for all invitees (it's a good idea to get e-mail addresses as well so that you can easily follow up with anyone who doesn't RSVP on time)
- ❏ Purchase/make guest favors; obtain packaging/wrapping for favors

Four to Eight Weeks Before

- ❏ Finalize the menu; if you and cohosts plan to do the cooking, determine who will prepare which dishes
- ❏ Address and mail invitations (four weeks in advance of the shower)
- ❏ Create a log to keep track of RSVPs
- ❏ Check in with cohosts regarding progress, delegate any new tasks that have arisen, and/or redistribute tasks as necessary
- ❏ Order a cake, if you're getting one from a bakery
- ❏ Order flowers for the shower
- ❏ Obtain your gift and card and the joint bridesmaids' gift (optional) for the bride

Two Weeks Before

- ❏ Follow up with guests who have not responded to the invitation
- ❏ Obtain decorations
- ❏ Obtain decorative and sturdy disposable plates, napkins, flatware, cups, tablecloths, etc., if you're going this route
- ❏ Acquire gift log
- ❏ Finalize games to be played, and acquire any necessary supplies for them
- ❏ Decide what you're going to wear; take the outfit to the dry cleaner, or iron if necessary

One Week Before

- ❏ Give the final head count to the site manager or caterer, if applicable; confirm other details with the site (table configuration, time you'll arrive to start setting up, etc.)
- ❏ Confirm the rental items and delivery time, if applicable
- ❏ Confirm any order for food being delivered or picked up, if applicable
- ❏ Shop for ingredients if you're preparing the food, as well as beverages and supplies (toilet paper, facial tissues, garbage bags) if the shower is being held at someone's home
- ❏ Prepare any food items that can be frozen, if applicable
- ❏ Wrap the favors
- ❏ Select desired background music (should be soft enough that it won't interfere with conversation)
- ❏ Purchase film and an extra camera battery
- ❏ Pick up any china, flatware, or serving dishes being borrowed for the shower

Two Days Before

- ❑ Clean your home, if the shower is at your place
- ❑ Purchase ice and any perishables that you couldn't pick up earlier
- ❑ Check the weather report; if it's an outdoor event and inclement weather threatens, put plan B into action; if the location is changing due to the weather, inform the guests; for an indoor event, make sure you have a place to stash umbrellas, boots, and wet raincoats

One Day Before

- ❑ If the shower is at your home, make preparations for the spaces in which you'll be entertaining guests (set up chairs, put breakable objects away, determine where you'll be serving the food, etc.)
- ❑ Decorate
- ❑ Check in with those picking up catered food and taking care of other last-minute items
- ❑ Have your nails done

Day of Shower

- ❑ Pick up or receive delivery of catered food, if applicable; pick up or receive rental items (this might occur the day before the shower instead)
- ❑ Set up as necessary (prepare food that couldn't be made earlier; put out plates, flatware, napkins, etc.; arrange place cards; put up final decorations; have gift log ready to go)
- ❑ Get dressed (give yourself enough time to primp)
- ❑ Have fun!

Details, Details

Ironing out the details in advance of the shower will help keep the party running smoothly. Be sure to consider the following points.

※ If the event is at someone's home, how and when will food be served? Will everything be buffet-style? If so, where will you set it all up, and who will be responsible for refilling platters? If you won't be having a buffet, who will do the serving?

※ If the shower is being held at someone's home, is there enough room in the refrigerator for all of the food?

※ Where will guests put their gifts for the bride?

※ Where will guests put their coats?

※ Will any special arrangements need to be made to accommodate certain guests (perhaps the bride's grandmother)?

※ Where will the bride sit?

※ Who will take pictures during the party?

※ Who will be in charge of changing the music during the party?

※ When will gifts be opened?

※ Who will be in charge of collecting wrapping paper and other trash?

※ Who will record who gave what to the bride?

※ Who will make the ribbon bouquet?

※ When will you start the games, and who will lead them?

※ How will favors be distributed? Will you hand them out, or will guests take their own from a table or basket as they leave?

※ Who will help the bride transport gifts home at the end of the event, and who will remain behind to help clean up?

ORGANIZATIONAL LIFESAVER

EVERYONE SHELLING OUT MONEY FOR THE SHOWER SHOULD SAVE ALL receipts, jotting down the item or service purchased at the top. Stash the receipts in an envelope so that you don't lose them. This will help everyone keep track of spending, as well as simplify matters when the time comes to divvy up expenses.

SHOWER BUDGET WORKSHEET

The worksheet on the next page has been provided to help you formulate a shower budget and keep track of expenses. Use it according to your needs, and cross off those elements that don't pertain to your particular situation. Use the first two columns for the total budget and the last two for your individual portion of the tab. Remember to account for gratuities, which can come into play if you're having food, rental items, or flowers delivered; if wait staff will be serving; or if you're hosting at a restaurant or club with a coat check and/or valet parking.

EXPENSE	TOTAL COST		INDIVIDUAL SHARE	
	Estimated	Actual	Estimated	Actual
Location fee				
Food				
Cake				
Beverages				
Ice				
Rental items				
Serving supplies (disposable plates, cups, napkins, tablecloth, etc.)				
Place cards				
Decorations (flowers, candles, etc.)				
Supplies for games				
Prizes				
Favors				
Packaging/wrapping for favors				
Entertainment				
Invitations				
Postage for invitations				
Gift for bride				
Bridesmaids' group gift for bride				
Gift log				
Scrapbook/photo album for bride				
Parking/transportation				
Travel expenses/accommodations				
Other				
TOTAL				

The Fun Stuff: Terrific Themes

Below are a variety of themes, some new, others tried-and-true. Use them to spark your imagination. Combine several (if the bride loves to cook *and* travel, think "foods from around the world"), put a new spin on one, or invent your own. Avoid complicated ideas that might confuse guests or turn gift-buying into a source of anxiety. (For tips on how to go about assigning certain aspects of the theme to guests, see All About Invitations on page 77.)

Gift-Related Themes

Around-the-clock shower: Each guest is assigned an hour of the day and purchases a corresponding gift—a set of juice glasses or a breakfast tray for 8:00 A.M., his-and-hers pajamas for midnight. Gifts are opened as a day would unfold.

Around-the-calendar shower: This is similar to the around-the-clock shower, except each guest brings a present that corresponds to a certain month or season. If you have a large group, simply assign the same month to multiple guests.

Around-the-house shower: Each guest brings a gift for a different room of the home—towels for the bathroom, a coffeemaker for the kitchen, a vase for the living area, garden implements for the yard.

Alphabet shower: Each guest is assigned a different letter of the alphabet and buys a gift beginning with that letter. Another option: Rather than going straight through the alphabet, have the letters chosen spell out a significant word or, perhaps, the groom's name.

Lingerie shower: Guests bring sexy or elegant undergarments, massage oil, and other tokens to heighten wedding-night passion. Some brides consider it great fun; others are mortified—as are quite a few mothers and grandmothers. Consider the average age and temperament of the guests before choosing this theme.

Pampering shower: Guests bring fragrant bath oils, gift certificates for massages and special spa treatments, and other indulgences to help the bride unwind and rejuvenate after all that hard work involved in planning the wedding.

Entertainment shower: Guests bring board games, movie passes, popcorn poppers, cocktail glasses, martini shakers, espresso makers, and anything else related to entertainment or entertaining.

Travel shower: Guests bring gifts targeted to the couple's footloose lifestyle, such as a travel alarm clock, leather-bound travel journal, or stocked toiletry kit for making air travel more comfortable. If the bride and groom are already well equipped in this area, try a globe-trotting shower in which each gift is linked to a different destination the couple hopes to visit.

Culinary shower: Guests bring items related to cooking or the kitchen to help the bride outfit a new home or to encourage her passion for cooking. As a special touch, buy a decorative recipe file box and ask each guest to bring a favorite recipe written on an index card (be sure to specify the size).

Activity-Related Themes

Jack-and-Jill shower: Both bride and groom attend, and both male and female guests are invited. The venue, menu, games, and activities usually reflect the coed crowd. Gift themes that work well include entertainment and travel, as well as ones that center on a shared hobby or favorite pastime.

Sports and leisure shower: Perfect for energetic couples, this party usually involves active diversions—for instance, a casual picnic and softball game for the guests in a local park (a backup for inclement weather could be an indoor picnic and a showing of *Bull Durham*). Other possibilities include a round of miniature golf, a trip to the bowling alley, or a visit to the batting cages followed by dinner in a historic brewpub. Gifts support the theme—anything from camping gear to tickets to a baseball game.

Wine shower: Arrange for a tasting at a nearby wine shop or vineyard, or find out if a local wine shop will send a staff member to conduct a tasting at your own home (make sure guests don't drink and drive). Guests bring a favorite vintage to fill out the couple's wine cellar or a wine-related gift. Specialty wine shops and catalogs offer loads of options, from decanters to coffee-table books on wine.

Inventing Your Own Theme

Use your imagination and your knowledge of the bride's personality to inspire a one-of-a-kind theme custom-made for her. Weave it into every element of the day, from gifts to games. Here are a few examples.

※ If the bride is famous for her love of warm weather, try a hot and spicy theme with fiery hors d'oeuvres, Bloody Marys made with pepper-infused vodka, salsa and samba music, and bright red decorative accents. Sprinkle heart-shaped red-hot candies over the table. Gifts could revolve around romance and passion, such as satin sheets, candlesticks for an intimate dinner, or a book of "adult" games. For favors, give gourmet hot sauces or massage oil (whichever take on "hot" you want to go with). Create a steamy version of bridal trivia with questions about everything from the bride's favorite tropical vacation spot to (if you think the bride and guests won't be terribly offended) her favorite part of the groom's anatomy.

✳ If she's a lifelong Anglophile heading to London on her honeymoon, host an afternoon tea with scones, clotted cream, miniature sandwiches, and bite-size sweets. Use a computer graphics program to design invitations featuring a teacup, the Union Jack, or a red telephone booth. Invent your own *Name That Tune* game by playing bits of famous love songs from the British Invasion and asking people to identify the titles and/or groups. Or read famous passages about love penned by well-known British poets and novelists (Shakespeare, Shelley, the Brontës, etc.) and have guests guess the authors. Another option: Create a vocabulary quiz asking guests to identify the American equivalents of British words, such as biscuits (cookies), crisps (potato chips), chips (French fries), and so on. Tying gifts to the theme should be easy. If she's that enamored with England, she may have registered for a china pattern from a British company like Spode, Wedgwood, or Royal Doulton (gifts, however, don't need to correspond with the theme). For favors, you could order tins of chocolate chip or oatmeal biscuits from the website of the famous London department store Harrods.

✳ If the bride lives for the eighties, take everyone on a trip back in time. Put Duran Duran and Cyndi Lauper on the stereo; decorate with posters of Tom Cruise, Rob Lowe, and other eighties heartthrobs; and create a pop culture trivia game revolving around that decade. Anything goes for food. For favors, you could hand out Rubik's Cubes or compilations of eighties tunes. Gifts could be DVDs of favorite eighties flicks, retro video games, and novelty items that are sure to sweep the bride up in a wave of nostalgia. (Tying the gifts into this theme is better if the bride already has most of what she needs; otherwise, you might want to limit the theme to the music and games so that the bride ends up with more traditional presents.)

Shower Games

The possibilities range from such old stalwarts as having guests fashion wedding gowns from toilet paper (the bride judges the winner) to more innovative diversions such as a name-that-love-song quiz (the host plays snippets of famous love songs, and guests guess the title and artist). Of course, you don't have to play games, but if you think the bride and guests would enjoy them, here are a few fresh ideas.

Famous Romances: This takes some effort on the part of the hosts, but it's great fun—especially for an entertainment shower. Come up with a list of twenty famous couples (real or fictional) and write clues to their identity. (Clue: She was a pampered pet; he was a lovable mutt from the wrong side of the tracks. Answer: Lady and the Tramp.) Read the clues aloud, and ask guests to write down the answers. The person who correctly identifies the most couples wins (be sure to have a few challenging ones on hand for tiebreakers). You could also compile a list of famous love-song lyrics or quotations from films or literature, read the first half of each aloud, and ask guests to finish the line. (Example: Rhett Butler tells Scarlett in *Gone with the Wind,* "Frankly, my dear...." Answer: "I don't give a damn.")

Who Am I?: Each guest receives a 3 x 5-inch card with her invitation and is asked to write down a memory of a special time she spent with the bride. At the shower, the host reads the cards aloud to the bride, who guesses each author's identity (this game is not for the shy bride). Afterward, the cards are placed in a scrapbook for the bride.

Toss the Bouquet: Make bouquets out of silk flowers tied with ribbon and have each guest toss one over her shoulder toward a target. Whoever gets closest wins. This activity works best outside or in a large room (be sure to remove any breakable objects from the space).

Bridal Bingo: Create "Bridal Bingo" cards, each bearing a grid with twenty-five empty spaces (five across, five down). Ask guests to jot down in these spaces items that they think the bride will receive as gifts. As she opens her presents, guests make an X over the presents they've gotten right. A row of five correct guesses translates to bingo.

Clothespins Revisited: Spice up that most traditional of shower games by putting a new spin on it. The basic rules are as follows: Each guest is given a clothespin to fasten onto her clothing when she arrives and is briefed on a list of taboo words chosen by the host (usually such bound-to-be-uttered words as "wedding," "honeymoon," "marriage," etc.). Whenever someone slips and says a forbidden word, she's out of the game and must surrender her clothespin to the person who caught her. The woman with the greatest number of clothespins at the end of the shower wins a prize. That's all well and good, but who wants to spend the afternoon looking like they've just lost a fight with the laundry? To make it more fun—and to give your guests more incentive to play along—scrap the clothespins in favor of a more desirable item. For a garden shower, give everyone a long-stemmed rose or a carnation (flower shops can provide small, no-spill plastic vials of water to preserve each bloom's freshness); this way, the winner will have a full bouquet as a parting gift. Make the prize a vase. For a pampering shower, you could purchase a variety of inexpensive "healing bead" bracelets, each in a different color. Make the prize a coordinating multicolored necklace including every type of bead in the bracelets.

Bridal Trivia: Like the clothespins game, this is an oldie, but it can be a goodie with a little imagination and effort on your part. Here's how it works. The host creates a list of multiple choice or fill-in-the-blank questions about the bride for the group to answer in writing. For example: Where did the couple meet? Where was their first date? How did the groom propose? The person to get the greatest number of answers right wins. To jazz up this old standard, use the shower theme to inspire the questions. A sample question for a culinary shower might read like this: We all know what a wonderful cook Anne is, but the first time she made dinner for Ron she was so nervous that she (a) burned an entire pot roast and had to call the fire department to put out the flames, (b) dropped the coq au vin she'd made all over his lap, (c) got the ingredients mixed up and served him an apple pie with a cup of salt and a pinch of sugar. You might have to get input from the bride, the groom, or your cohosts to compile a long enough list (aim for twelve to twenty questions), but you're sure to pique your guests' interest and teach them a thing or two about the bride. Hint: Try to throw in questions that span her entire life so neither childhood friends nor newer acquaintances will feel left out. Prepare a bonus question or two in case of a tie.

Wedding Whites: Here's another great game for a food-lovers' fest. Fill and number a dozen clear sealable storage bags with white cooking ingredients (sugar, baking soda, flour, confectioner's sugar, and so on). Give numbered slips of paper to all of your guests, then pass around the bags; without opening the bags, each guest writes down what she thinks the contents are. The person to correctly identify the greatest number of substances wins a cooking-related prize (perhaps some inexpensive but handy kitchen gadget). For a different approach, fill numbered paper cups with various fresh herbs. Cover them in aluminum foil, and poke holes in the top. Guests sniff each and guess the herb.

EYE ON THE PRIZE

PLAN TO SPEND BETWEEN $5 AND $15 ON EACH PRIZE depending on your budget and the number of prizes you're buying. A small picture frame, a box of pretty note cards, or sachets will do nicely. You can also link prizes to the theme. To save money, have flowers perform double duty as decorations and awards. Prizes can be handed out or put in a basket from which the winner picks her own. Be sure to buy a few extras in case of a tie.

More Bridal Fun

Ribbon bouquet: A common shower activity is to save the bows and ribbons from the presents and combine them into a mock bouquet, usually by threading the ribbons through a hole poked into a paper plate and taping the bows to the plate (a doily may be used instead). This pseudo-bouquet is then carried by the bride during the rehearsal. Other twists include turning the ribbons and bows into a hat or boa to be worn at the bachelorette party.

Gift log: It's good manners (not to mention an indispensable service to the bride) to keep a log of the presents she receives; this not only provides her with a wonderful keepsake, but also makes it easier for her to write thank-you notes. One person should be designated to fill in the log during the shower. As the bride opens each present, write down the name of the giver as well as the specific items given. You can make your own gift-log book or purchase a ready-made one.

Wishing well: This old-fashioned tradition can accompany any theme. The host constructs a decorative "well" out of a cardboard box and festoons it with bows and ribbon. A similar contraption can be created by decorating a new kitchen trash pail, putting a new mop and broom on either side of it, and connecting the resulting two "posts" with crepe paper. Fancier wishing wells can be rented from party supply centers. Guests place small, useful wrapped items such as wooden spoons, scissors, and candles in the well as supplements to their primary gifts. (If you decide to incorporate this activity into the shower plans, you'll obviously need to give guests a heads-up when you invite them so they'll come prepared.) Keep in mind that if the bride lives on her own, she probably has a lot of this stuff; you don't want to load her down with a bunch of items she doesn't need. A twist on this tradition is for each guest to write down a piece of relationship advice for the bride and put it in the well. If you go this route, place colorful index cards or a small pad of colorful paper next to the well, along with a few pens. After the shower, you can put the words of wisdom in a scrapbook for the bride.

Thoughtful Touches

Create a shower scrapbook: Put a keepsake invitation on the opening page, and ask each guest to write her wishes for the couple on a page inside. Or have each person bring a small token that signifies a special memory she shares with the bride and an accompanying description—a postcard from a trip the two took to Hawaii after college, a ticket stub from a favorite play they saw together, or a written anecdote. Paste them all into the scrapbook along with photos from the shower.

Put together a pocket-size photo album: Take pictures at the shower, print them out, and put them in a small album for the bride. Or take Polaroid snapshots at the party, and ask each guest to write a brief note on the picture of herself to slip into the album.

Compose a poem about the bride: Read it aloud to her, with each bridesmaid reciting a verse. Print a written copy in an attractive font on a high quality paper, and frame it for her as a keepsake. Or, if you and the other bridesmaids can carry a tune, compose personalized lyrics to one of the bride's favorite songs and belt them out to her.

Make a video: This is a somewhat ambitious endeavor, but it makes a wonderful keepsake. The project works best when the bridesmaids are friends who would actually enjoy spending a few weekend afternoons together revisiting significant spots in the bride's life (her high school, the ice cream parlor where she worked as a teen, the country house she was renting when she met the groom) and gathering comments from former teachers, coaches, and so on.

Give her a break: If you want to help the bride in the busy weeks leading up to the wedding, tell her she doesn't need to send you a thank-you note.

Spare her the details: If you let the bride in on the planning, don't burden her with bulletins on RSVPs, logistics, or discord among the cohosts.

REFLECTIONS FROM REAL BRIDES

"I didn't want a big shower, so my bridesmaids surprised me with an afternoon tea for a dozen close friends and family members. They found this charming little tearoom that had a whimsical, Alice in Wonderland–inspired decor. My maid of honor bought a journal with pictures of teapots on it and had everyone write a personalized message on a different page. Underneath that, she jotted down the gift they'd brought. Inside the front cover, she glued one of the invitations—shaped like a teacup, of course.**"**

—ANNE MONROE

Favor Ideas

The usual suspects are pampering products, miniature desktop accessories, and sweets, but there are countless options. Use the shower's theme to guide you, and note that favors can also do double duty as decorations. Here are a few suggestions.

- ❊ Fancy soaps (wrap a trio of small bars in tulle, and tie with ribbon for extra flair)
- ❊ Scented candles tied with raffia
- ❊ Packets of seeds (perfect for a garden shower)
- ❊ Small flowering plants in terra-cotta pots (let these double as decorations by clustering them to form a breakaway centerpiece)
- ❊ Brushed metal tins filled with mini–cookie cutters (link the shapes to the theme)
- ❊ Packets of gourmet herbal tea
- ❊ Decorative jars of jam or preserves (wrap in gingham for a homespun touch)
- ❊ Packages of scone, muffin, or bread mix (grits mix for a Southern bride, sourdough bread mix for a San Francisco native)
- ❊ Decorative corkscrews or stoppers for a shower with a wine theme
- ❊ Bags of chocolate-covered coffee beans

Chapter Six

Girls Just Want to Have Fun
The Bachelorette Party and Bridesmaids' Luncheon

Generally smaller and more casual than the bridal shower, the bachelorette party serves as a last hurrah for the bride, a chance to bid farewell to her days as a singleton in style. The tradition was born as a feminist answer to the bachelor party—a rite of passage invented by the ancient Greeks. Some brides' friends treat them to a day at a spa, others indulge in a weekend of revelry in Vegas, and still others unwind with a cozy night curled up on the couch watching favorite flicks. The goal is to give all involved a chance to let their hair down, share some laughs, and wax nostalgic—all while helping the bride temporarily forget the stress of wedding planning and remember what fun friends she has. Celebrate in whatever style makes her happy, whether it involves G-ratings or G-strings.

Bachelorette Basics

Who hosts? Usually the bridesmaids plan the party as a group, with the maid of honor in the lead role, but any close friend of the bride can take the helm. If the maid of honor did most of the work on the shower, a well-organized bridesmaid might politely offer to take charge of this event to ease her load.

When should the party take place? Most bachelorette parties are scheduled one to three weeks before the wedding, though you're free to set an earlier date for a weekend getaway or a later one if the bride's friends won't be in town until a few days before the wedding weekend. One caveat: Don't schedule it the night before an important event such as the bridal portrait sitting, the rehearsal, or the wedding itself, where dark circles and dragging feet would be undesirable. The timing of the bachelorette party often coincides with the bachelor party to keep the bride from sitting home worrying about what her fiancé is up to.

What kind of party should it be? Any kind you think will please the bride, as long as it's affordable and not too complicated to organize. Like the shower, this event does not need to be a surprise, so if you're uncertain what type to plan, ask the guest of honor. Maybe there's an activity she loves but her fiancé loathes. If she still dreams about her disco days but he won't be caught dead on the dance floor, go club hopping. Or, if the couple prefers a coed event, organize a joint bachelor/ bachelorette bash hosted by the bridesmaids and groomsmen.

Who's invited? There·are no hard-and-fast rules regarding who is invited to the bachelorette party, except that all of the bridesmaids should be included, as should any of the bride's sisters who are old enough to join in the fun. Women who are performing a special role in the ceremony, such as giving a reading, are also usu- ally included if they are around the bride's age, as are sisters of the groom if the bride is quite friendly with them. Close friends of the bride are often included as well. Relatives around the same age as the bride and groom can make the guest list if they are on close terms with the couple, as can close coworkers. Mothers and older relatives are generally included only at the bride's request. The average group ranges from about six to fifteen people, though some parties—particularly coed bashes—are much larger. Take into account the logistics when drawing up your guest list; a club might easily accommodate two dozen friends, but you'd need a home theater to accommodate them all for a night watching Julia Roberts movies.

Are handwritten invitations necessary? No. The phone or e-mail is fine, though if you want to mail casual invitations that reflect the party's theme, by all means do so. If you'll need a final head count, give everyone a cutoff date for RSVPs. Also note any special dress requirements. If you're planning a day at the beach followed by a seafood dinner, remind guests to bring a change of clothes, a light sweater, and shoes (unless the restaurant is ultra-casual, it will probably frown on flip-flops).

Who pays? Most bachelorette parties are divided evenly among the bridesmaids or all of the guests, with everyone chipping in extra to cover the bride's portion and, perhaps, a group gift. The cardinal rule is to handle the bill discreetly. The last thing the bride needs is to see her friends haggling over the tab. Ask for set contributions ahead of time or have people reimburse you later. If a more lavish celebration is being planned, the idea should be discussed among the bridesmaids and other participants ahead of time to find out if everyone is willing to splurge. If a bridesmaid can't attend, don't ask her to chip in.

GRACIOUS GESTURES

IF YOU CAN'T ATTEND THE BACHELORETTE PARTY but want to make a contribution, find out when and where the party will take place. If the venue is a restaurant or bar, have a bottle of wine or champagne sent to the table with your compliments. If the event will be held at someone's home, send flowers.

THINGS TO DO CHECKLIST

The following list is a general outline of the steps involved in putting together a bachelorette bash. Use it according to your needs, and cross out those elements that don't pertain to your situation.

- ❑ Ask the bride if she wants a bachelorette party and, if so, what type
- ❑ Discuss with the other bridesmaids how planning responsibilities and costs will be divided.
- ❑ Pick a date
- ❑ Put together the guest list
- ❑ Select a venue—or venues
- ❑ Make any necessary reservations for the site(s)
- ❑ Send save-the-date notices by mail or e-mail for a weekend destination event
- ❑ For a weekend event, make travel arrangements and book accommodations (you may book a block of rooms or have each guest make her own reservations)
- ❑ For a weekend event, make arrangements for transportation in and around destination locale
- ❑ Make arrangements for entertainment, if applicable
- ❑ Reserve rental items, if necessary
- ❑ Arrange for transportation for guests for bachelorette event (see page 103)
- ❑ Invite guests (by mail, phone, or e-mail)
- ❑ Decide on games and gag gifts; if necessary, acquire corresponding supplies
- ❑ Follow up with invitees who have not responded
- ❑ Confirm reservations for venue, travel, accommodations, transportation, rentals, and entertainment
- ❑ Pick up/receive rental items, if applicable
- ❑ Other _____
- ❑ Other _____
- ❑ Other _____
- ❑ Other _____

Timing Is Everything

❊ If you're holding an informal, local event, you can extend invitations anywhere from two weeks to one month before the party; if you need to give a site a final head count, extend the invitations on the earlier side of this time frame. Note, too, that if you're inviting any out-of-towners, you should let them know far enough in advance that they'll be able to make travel arrangements should they wish to attend; give them a call, or send a save-the-date notice as early as possible.

❊ If you're planning a casual destination event (say, a weekend at a friend's country house that's only a drive away), let people know a month in advance so they can clear their calendars.

❊ For more lavish events that require booking flights and reserving hotel rooms, let everyone know three to four months in advance; if it's peak season at the destination, you might need to take this step even earlier. For such an extravaganza, it's a good idea to call people, see if they're interested in participating, and then go over the details with those who wish to attend.

Friendship is a sheltering tree.
— Samuel Taylor Coleridge

BACHELORETTE BUDGET WORKSHEET

The following worksheet outlines the expenditures that can come into play when throwing a bachelorette bash. This is a general guideline only; not all of the elements detailed here will apply to every situation, so use the worksheet according to your needs. In the first two columns you can fill in total costs; in the last two, you can fill in each individual's share when costs are divided. Don't forget to account for gratuities (for wait staff, chauffeur, parking, entertainment, and deliveries).

EXPENSE	TOTAL COST		INDIVIDUAL SHARE	
	Estimated	Actual	Estimated	Actual
Location fee				
Food				
Drinks				
Entertainment				
Rental items				
Party supplies				
Items for games				
Gag gifts for bride				
Transportation service				
Travel/accommodations				
Other				
Other				
Other				
TOTAL				

Getting There and Back—Safely

Bachelorette parties frequently involve at least a cocktail or two all around, so if you're planning anything other than a slumber party at home, you'll need to give some thought to transportation.

※ Consider hiring a limo, a car service, or another mode of chauffeured transportation. Get creative and book a trolley, an old-fashioned school bus, or a vintage car. Or take the most affordable route—public transit.

※ If one of the guests offers to play designated driver ahead of time, be absolutely sure she wants to do it and can be trusted to abstain for the evening.

※ Pay attention to how much guests are drinking. If anyone is not in any condition to drive home, offer to let her spend the night if the party is at your place, call her a cab or car service, or find a sober guest to take her home. Do this if you have the slightest suspicion that someone has had one too many, and insist that she go along with one of these suggestions if she resists. Not only would it be tragic if someone were involved in a car accident, but the party's host could be held legally responsible.

Themes and Settings

Like bridal showers and weddings themselves, bachelorette parties have evolved into highly personalized events, with themes tailored to the guest of honor's tastes in entertainment, food, drinks—you name it. You can take the traditional route, toasting her at local hot spots; whisk her off for a glamorous weekend getaway if finances allow; or travel no farther than your own cozy living room for an old-fashioned sleepover. Use your imagination to craft a night (or an afternoon or morning) custom-made to fit her idea of a great time.

Out and About

Thrills and chills: Take the bride to an amusement park. Screaming at the top of her lungs on a roller coaster will give her the perfect release for all of that pent-up frustration about the seating chart.

Epicurean extravaganza: Book a table at a four-star restaurant and go all out with a multi-course meal.

Seasonal adventure: Plan an activity that makes the most of the season: an apple-picking excursion, a visit to a pick-your-own pumpkin patch, or a hayride in the fall; sledding or cross-country skiing followed by hot chocolate in the winter; a day of bronzing by the pool followed by tropical drinks in the summer; a tour through a garden or a field trip to a baseball game in the spring.

Sports-lovers' affair: If the bride and groom are outdoor types, consider anything from a day at the batting cages, miniature golf, or rock climbing at a local health club to a weekend of camping, canoeing, and kayaking. Make it a just-girls outing or invite the guys along. For a kitschy twist, try roller skating or bowling (glow-in-the-dark if you can find it).

Boatload of fun: For a small group, charter a small boat and spend an afternoon cruising. Being on the water provides the perfect escape for the bride who wants to get away from it all for a few hours. Make sure everyone has sunscreen!

High rollers' heaven: Spend an afternoon at the racetrack with lunch in the club-house, or a night at the nearest casino (drinks are free, and you can take in a show while you're there). Or go all out and head to Vegas or Atlantic City for the weekend. Be sure to provide the bride with a roll of lucky quarters for the slot machines.

Spa central: Spas are a splurge, but basking in mud baths or sea-salt tubs can be heaven on earth—and a great way to bond with the other bridesmaids. As a more affordable alternative, book a local nail salon exclusively for your group for a few hours of pedicures and manicures (or see the at-home take on this type of event below).

Her heart's desire: Plan a weekend getaway that revolves around the bride's biggest passion (other than the groom). If she's a shopaholic, spend two days meandering along Chicago's Miracle Mile or Manhattan's Fifth Avenue. If she's crazy about culture and history, head to D.C. to check out the exhibits at the Smithsonian and visit the monuments.

Night on the town: Take her to a comedy club, a karaoke bar, a rock concert, the theater, the symphony, a poetry slam—wherever she'd love to go with the girls on a Saturday night.

Home Sweet Home

Home spa: Stock up on nail files, toe separators, hand cream, peppermint foot lotion, and a variety of nail polishes so that guests can give each other manicures and pedicures or do their own nails; tell everyone to bring their flip-flops. You might also purchase soothing facial scrubs and cooling eye masks, or whip up your own homemade versions. For cool refreshment, offer a variety of delicious smoothies and set out pitchers of ice water (lemon slices add a nice touch). If you're going for the health spa effect, munchies can be dried fruits and unsalted nuts. Or make your spa about pure, luxurious indulgence, and splurge on champagne and truffles; another alternative is to make chocolate fondue and offer plenty of strawberries, as well as sliced pineapple, banana, and apple for dipping. Play New Age music and burn fragrant candles for extra ambiance.

Pajama party: Include all of the staples—truth or dare, girl talk, and plenty of junk food. If you want to get a little fancy, put together a make-your-own-sundae bar. Rummage through your old cassette tapes or CDs for nostalgic tunes bound to give the bride flashbacks of her misspent youth, and rent a bunch of her favorite films (be sure to make popcorn).

Boys' night: There's nothing that says a gathering of women has to be girly. Plan a stereotypical boys' night, complete with poker, scotch, cigars, and if you so choose, a stripper or a steamy film.

Family-style dinner: If you've got room, invite everyone over—girls and guys—for a backyard barbecue or an all-you-can-eat spaghetti extravaganza. Be sure to add atmospheric touches: country music and a washtub of ice-cold longnecks for the barbecue; red-and-white checkered tablecloths, jugs of red wine, and Frank Sinatra tunes for the pasta fest. If you're lucky enough to have a big yard or large living room, hire an instructor to give the guests a line-dancing lesson after the ribs and chicken. Another means of entertainment is to have everyone give a toast—humorous or heartfelt (give the participants some advance notice so they'll come prepared). In the midst of such festivities, even the most reserved guests usually get into the spirit.

REFLECTIONS FROM REAL BRIDES

❝The day before my wedding, my bridesmaids treated me to a girls' day out— to have my nails done, to relax over a really great lunch, and to do last-minute shopping. It was just the four of us, and I really appreciated that.❞

—ELENI SHIPE

Games Mother Never Taught You

First Kiss: The bride kicks this one off by telling the story of the first time she and her fiancé ever locked lips. Then each guest has the choice of sharing the story of her first smooch with her significant other or her first smooch ever. Vote on the most romantic, funniest, and steamiest. Bonus round: Have everyone recount their best and worst kisses ever. If you're including presents in the festivities, it's fun to ask each participant to describe her idea of the perfect romantic evening and to bring something for the bride that echoes it.

Catch the Bridal Bouquet: Cut out a photo of a bouquet from a bridal magazine, and attach it to a dartboard. Each player gets three chances to hit the flowers with a dart; the closest to the bull's-eye wins (and will be the next to get married). Another option: Substitute a cutout of a gorgeous male model or movie star for the flowers.

Brief Encounters: Each partygoer buys a pair of underwear for the bride. Encourage some to select skimpy thongs, others to shop for whimsical polka-dot panties, and others to find quirky or comical items (men's boxers, grandma-style underwear, and so on). If you're going out, ask everyone to wrap the undies. If you're staying in, string them up on a clothesline. Then have the bride guess who brought which pair.

THE BLUSHING BRIDE

IT IS TRADITIONAL TO GENTLY EMBARRASS THE BRIDE, but remember that you're there to help her relax, not humiliate her. Any teasing should be good-natured. If she doesn't want to wear a veil or ask a strange man for his boxers, don't make her do it. If she bristles at being the butt of jokes, you're better off abandoning all efforts to make her turn red. On the other hand, if she adores being the center of attention, pile on the fake tiaras and condom leis, and encourage cute guys to serenade her.

The Bridesmaids' Luncheon

What is it? Long before bachelorette parties came into vogue, this was the standard ladies' prewedding get-together. Today, many brides host such a gathering—whether it be lunch, brunch, or dinner—to thank attendants for their help. Some opt instead for an activity such as a group trip to a nail salon—bride's treat.

When does it take place? Usually a day or two before the wedding, when all of the bridesmaids are in town for the big event.

What should I wear? Bridesmaids' luncheons tend to be dressy-casual rather than formal, but if you're invited to one, inquire about the appropriate attire.

Should I bring a gift? The only instance in which you'd bring a present is if you and the other bridesmaids are using this opportunity to give the bride a group gift (a scrapbook, for instance). Otherwise, gifts are not given to the bride (this is, after all, her chance to thank you). Many brides take this opportunity to present the bridesmaids with tokens of appreciation.

Is there anything I need to do? Show up and enjoy yourself!

Chapter Seven

Travel, Transportation, and Accommodations

I f the wedding isn't local, among your first orders of business should be making arrangements to get there and finding a place to stay. Careful planning and attention to detail will keep you safe en route and get you to the church (or wherever the wedding is being held) not only on time, but looking radiant and relaxed as well.

THINGS TO DO CHECKLIST
- ❑ Make arrangements to get to wedding destination (book flight, rent car, purchase train or bus tickets, have own car tuned up, or firm up plans to have another driver pick you up)
- ❑ Book hotel room, or make plans to stay with someone
- ❑ Arrange for transportation to and from airport/station at point of origin
- ❑ Arrange for transportation to and from airport/station at destination
- ❑ Make arrangements to get to and from rehearsal and wedding

❑ Make plans for someone to take care of your pet, if applicable
❑ Confirm accommodations
❑ Confirm all travel arrangements

Wedding Travel Basics

※ Be forewarned that neither the bride nor her parents are expected to pay for your travel arrangements or your hotel room. That's your responsibility as a bridesmaid.

※ If the bride or her parents offer to cover your travel tab, you may graciously accept. If they are springing for you only (perhaps because you're in graduate school or traveling a greater distance than the other people in the party), don't mention their generosity to any of the other bridesmaids. Thank the bride or her family privately, and send them a handwritten note to reiterate your appreciation as soon as you get home. You might also send a basket of flowers or fruit, or a specialty item from your hometown.

※ If you'll need a hotel room, book it early, especially if the wedding will take place in a touristy spot in high season.

※ When making your hotel reservation, ask for a quiet room—one that isn't on the ground floor and doesn't face the street.

※ Bringing a date? Discuss who's going to pay for what—and, more importantly, who's going to sleep where—ahead of time.

※ Never make disparaging remarks to the bride or other bridesmaids about the price or quality of the accommodations—even in jest.

We are all travelers in the wilderness of this world, and the best we can find in our travels is an honest friend.

— Robert Louis Stevenson

Cost-Cutting Tips

✳ Many engaged couples reserve discounted blocks of hotel rooms or, at the very least, provide a list of hotels, inns, and B&Bs in various price ranges. Booking the hotel where the bride has reserved a block of rooms offers a number of advantages. Most likely, she's selected places that are convenient to the wedding venue and any other events that have been planned for out-of-towners. There's also a better chance that the lodgings will be up to decent standards. Moreover, you'll be able to bond with fellow guests, meet for breakfast or a drink at the hotel bar, and share a taxi.

✳ If you can't afford the hotel(s) the bride has suggested, find out whether another bridesmaid might want to share a room and split the cost.

✳ Another option is to ask the bride or a local member of the wedding party if there are more affordable options nearby. If that's too embarrassing, call the local convention and visitors bureau, the chamber of commerce, or AAA or another auto club if you're a member.

✳ As a last resort, find out whether one of the other bridesmaids who lives in the area has a spare room that she might be willing to offer you. (If you decide to go this route, follow the pointers on how to be the perfect houseguest on page 116.)

Getting There Is Half the Fun

There are numerous measures you can take to minimize problems and make your trip more comfortable. Check out the sections that pertain to your situation.

Clear Skies Ahead

❋ If you'll be flying, book your ticket well in advance of the wedding so that you have a better shot at the cheaper fares.

❋ Steer clear of super-saver flights that require multiple plane changes en route. Your stress level will be high enough without braving a ten-hour airplane odyssey and fretting over missed connections.

❋ If your schedule is flexible enough, try to choose a flight that arrives at least half a day before wedding events are scheduled to begin so a delay won't force you to miss anything important or cause you to arrive late, harried, and flustered.

❋ When you make your reservation, request the type of seat you want—aisle to make getting in and out easier, window if you want to sleep or take in the view, bulkhead (first row in the section) for more legroom. The earlier you make your seating arrangements, the more likely you are to get what you want.

❋ Check whether breakfast, lunch, or dinner is included in the flight. If not, bring some healthy snacks along. If food will be served, order a special meal or snack (vegetarian, low-fat, kosher, etc.). These meals don't cost extra, they tend to be fresher, and you usually get served first. (You may want to bring something to munch on anyway, in case you find the portions to be too small or the offerings to be less than appetizing.)

❋ Bring along a few lightweight items to make the flight more comfortable and to help you arrive looking fabulous. Include bottled water, lip balm, hand lotion, and face moisturizer, as planes tend to be very dry and it's easy to get dehydrated (purchase the water after you go through security, and make sure any liquids or lotions you pack in your carry-on adhere to the airport size guidelines and regulations). Another simple pleasure is a comfy pair of socks or slippers.

❋ Dress in layers on the plane, regardless of the climate in your point of origin or at your destination, as flights can be chilly at times. A good bet is a big, cozy shawl or pashmina that can do double duty as a blanket on the plane and as a stylish accessory once you're on terra firma. Choose a solid neutral such as black or taupe so you'll be able to toss it over your shoulders throughout the weekend as needed.

※ Do not check your bridesmaid dress or the outfit you plan to wear to the rehearsal dinner; carry them on the plane with you. The same goes for shoes, wraps, jewelry, and anything else the bride expects you to wear at the wedding. Tuck other items you can't do without or replace easily, such as extra contact lenses and any necessary medication, into your carry-on. It's a good idea to also include an extra pair of underwear and a toothbrush to tide you over in case your luggage gets lost or delayed.

※ It is advisable to carry your bridesmaid dress in a garment bag. Most passenger cabins have a small area near the front of the plane where garment bags can be hung, giving you a better chance of arriving wrinkle-free. So that you won't forget to collect the dress when you land, bring along a small pad of sticky notes; put one on the back of the seat in front of you and one on your purse to help you remember.

※ Bring a good book to help you relax on board. You might also want to bring a portable music player with headphones.

All Aboard: Traveling by Train or Bus

❋ Choose a bus or train that gets you into town well before you need to be there in case of delays; buses can get stuck in traffic, and trains can run behind schedule.

❋ Call ahead to find out whether there is someplace to hang a garment bag on board; if not, pack the dress in your suitcase carefully using the method described on page 119. Even if you're planning on hanging the dress on board, it's a good idea to bring some extra tissue paper with you; that way, if it turns out you're unable to hang the dress, you can fold it in half (with the tissue paper at the fold) and lay it down in the overhead storage.

❋ Bring food, something to drink, magazines, a portable music player with head-phones—anything that will help make your trip more enjoyable.

Ground Transportation

❋ Let the bride know when you'll be arriving in town, as it will most likely ease her mind and facilitate general planning if she has your itinerary. Plus, although you shouldn't count on it, she may want to have someone meet you at the airport or station and drive you to the hotel.

❋ Find out ahead of time whether shuttles or buses are available to get you where you need to go, how much they cost, and how often they run. If you're staying at a hotel, inquire if it offers shuttle service.

❋ If you plan to take a cab, make sure you've got enough cash on hand. You might not be able to find an ATM at the airport or station, or you may be too pressed for time to look for one.

In and Around Town

❋ The bride will probably arrange transportation to and from the rehearsal and the wedding for you, but to avoid any unpleasant surprises, it's best to ask ahead of time if you'll need to make arrangements.

- ※ If the bride is not organizing the transportation, ask local bridesmaids if you'll be able to hitch a ride.
- ※ Another option is to rent a car. If other bridesmaids are coming from out of town, you could play chauffeur and split the cost of the rental.
- ※ If you're not keen on driving and you're out of luck with local bridesmaids, look into the availability of taxis or car services.
- ※ Make sure you have directions to and from all of the places you need to be.

Road Trip

- ※ Leave yourself ample time to find your way and allow for unexpected traffic or road construction. Also, plan on giving yourself breaks to stretch your legs, grab a bite, and if it's a long haul, fill up on gas. If you're driving alone, plan to arrive an hour before sundown. That way, even if you get lost, you have a good chance of still making it to your destination in daylight.
- ※ If you're not bringing a date and don't want to make the trip alone, find out whether another bridesmaid or guest lives near you and might want to come along for the ride.
- ※ Make sure you have maps of all the areas you'll be traveling through; keep them somewhere within easy reach.
- ※ If you're not sure how to get to the hotel, call the front desk for directions.
- ※ If you're heading to a major metropolitan area, be prepared for parking charges at the hotel.
- ※ Bring emergency supplies: a fully charged cell phone and a charger, cash for repairs (not all towing services and auto shops accept credit cards), a flashlight with working batteries, a blanket, lots of bottled water, and an air canister for your tires. Consider buying an emergency car kit, available from AAA and auto supply stores. If you don't already belong, think about getting a AAA membership, which provides twenty-four-hour roadside assistance and free trip-planning advice.

※ Bring along plenty of music, books on tape, and munchies to keep you from getting bored and to minimize your stress level.

※ To keep your dress wrinkle-free, transport it in a garment bag; lay the bag flat along the back seat, or hang it from the hook behind the driver's seat (do the latter only if the dress won't block or compromise the driver's view). For more tips on packing your bridesmaid dress, see page 119.

House Calls

If you're considering staying at a fellow bridesmaid's house, make sure you won't be crashing on the floor or camping out at party central. You'll need a good night's sleep in order to be at your best when greeting guests, smiling for the photographer, and rescuing the bride from last-minute fiascoes.

How to Be the Houseguest from Heaven

※ Bring a gift for your host. Make it something small and lightweight if you've got to carry it on a plane. A hostess gift should have a personal touch whenever possible. If she's a Francophile, have a local wine shop help you select a good bottle of French wine, or buy a package of lavender sachets reminiscent of Provence. If you don't know anything about her tastes, choose a specialty item from your hometown—a box of the local chocolate shop's world-famous fudge, for instance.

※ If your host has young children, bring a small gift for each of them.

※ Keep your room neat while you're there, and leave it looking like you found it.

※ Hang up wet towels—do not leave them lying around.

※ Stay off the host's phone. Bring a cell phone, and keep your voice down when using it, especially late at night and early in the morning.

※ Replace whatever you use. Stop by a local grocery or convenience store and pick up fresh orange juice, milk, or muffins.

※ Send a handwritten thank-you note as soon as you get home.

How to Help if You're Local

※ Offer to scout out lodging options in the area and type up a list that the bride can send to those coming from out of town. You could also volunteer to let the happy couple put your contact information on the mailing so that they won't have to field questions.

※ Lend a hand by shuttling some out-of-town guests to and from the airport or station.

※ Offer to drive out-of-towners in the wedding party to the rehearsal dinner and back.

※ Put up another bridesmaid, if you have room and don't mind having a guest.

The Hostess with the Mostess

If another bridesmaid will be your guest, take these simple steps to ensure that everything goes smoothly—for your sake and hers.

※ Provide a clean and tidy space with a working alarm clock. Clear out a drawer, and make room in a closet (you don't want her wedding day outfit to get wrinkled).

※ The bathroom should also be clean. Leave some counter space for her toiletries, and provide her with a washcloth, hand towel, and bath towel.

※ The kitchen should be well stocked with beverages and snacks. Let your guest know where to find glasses, plates, and silverware.

※ Provide your guest with a set of house keys so that she can come and go when you're not there.

※ Encourage your guest to feel at home, but politely let her know about any ground rules: "The kids go to sleep at 10:00 P.M., so we all try to be quiet after that."

Packing Primer

❋ Opt for a soft-sided suitcase with wheels.

❋ Bring everything you usually use in your daily beauty regimen. If, like many bridesmaids, you feel less than enthusiastic about your dress, you'll want whatever you can get your hands on to help you look and feel gorgeous.

❋ If you're staying at a hotel and you'll need a hair dryer, call to find out if the room is equipped with one so that you don't have to lug yours in your suitcase.

❋ Find out if the bride and groom are planning extra outings—a few drinks after the rehearsal, a farewell brunch, and so on—and whether you'll need special attire for any of them. If you're unsure, go for dark colors (black can easily be dressed up or down) and lightweight layers in case it gets chilly or hot.

❋ Pack strategically to avoid wrinkles. Choose fabrics that travel well (blends instead of linen or cotton), fold garments carefully, and slip layers of tissue paper between each one. Fold clothes just enough to fit in your suitcase, and hang them up as soon as you arrive.

❋ Avoid traveling with valuable jewelry; all eyes will be on the bride anyway, so there's no need to risk losing your finest accessories.

❋ Make a list of all the items you'll need, including everything from the specific clothes you'll wear each day to toiletries and accessories to any wedding-related items, phone numbers, and directions. That way you will have less of a chance of leaving something behind. As you pack each article, check it off your list to keep track. (See page 120 for some items that you don't want to forget or overlook.)

Have Dress, Will Travel

The following packing tips will give you the best chance of having your dress arrive at the wedding destination sans wrinkles. The best way to carry the dress is in a garment bag, but tips for packing the gown in a suitcase are provided as well in case you absolutely must go this route. Once you arrive at your destination, unpack the dress immediately and hang it up in the closet, making sure there's plenty of space around it.

Garment Bag

1. Hang the dress on a padded hanger.
2. Stuff the dress with crinkled tissue paper to help it hold its shape.
3. Put the dress in an ordinary plastic dry-cleaning bag—the longest one you can find if it's a floor-length dress—and then place it in a lightweight, zippered garment bag (note, however, that you should not actually store your dress in plastic). Don't pack toiletries or anything else that might leak in the bag or even a side pocket.

Suitcase

1. If you must put your dress in a suitcase, fold it at the natural crease points (sleeves fold at the shoulders, bodice folds at the waist) and place several pieces of smooth tissue paper between the layers of fabric that have resulted from the folds. Make the fewest number of folds necessary for the outfit to fit in the suitcase.
2. Wrap the folded garment in another layer of tissue paper, and pack it between other items in the suitcase, making sure that it lies flat (even out the items below the dress).

IF THE SHOE FITS

So THAT YOUR SHOES ARRIVE AT THE WEDDING IN GOOD CONDITION, stuff them with socks to keep them from getting crushed. You should also put them in protective shoe bags (large-size kitchen storage bags make an affordable substitute) so that the outer part does not get marked up.

DON'T LEAVE HOME WITHOUT IT

Obviously, you need to bring your bridesmaid dress, wedding day accessories, and outfits for all wedding-related events, as well as clothes for downtime in between. The following list is simply intended to point out things that you might not think about or that could easily be overlooked.

- ❏ Invitations and directions to all events
- ❏ Plane, train, or bus tickets
- ❏ Hotel confirmation number
- ❏ Directions to place you'll be staying
- ❏ Notes for any toast you're making
- ❏ Headache relief medication, antacid tablets, tampons, and adhesive bandages (in case those new shoes cause blisters)
- ❏ Blotting tissues (so you don't have a shiny forehead in the formal portraits)
- ❏ Earplugs, eye mask, warm socks, or anything else to help you sleep comfortably
- ❏ Button-down shirt to wear when having hair and makeup done (so you won't ruin the stylist's work by pulling your shirt over your head later)
- ❏ Camera and extra camera batteries or your camera charger
- ❏ Extra nylons
- ❏ Clear nail polish (in case of stocking runs)
- ❏ Anything "old," "new," "borrowed," or "blue" you're supplying
- ❏ Cell phone
- ❏ Phone numbers at which other bridesmaids, the bride, and other key players can be reached during the wedding weekend
- ❏ Small notepad and pen to jot down information
- ❏ Small mirror to tuck in purse for quick makeup and hair checks
- ❏ Lightweight umbrella
- ❏ Comfy, casual clothes and shoes for the trip home
- ❏ Travel sewing kit

Chapter Eight

The Wedding Whirlwind

The wedding weekend is finally here. Whether you've been so immersed in the details that it seems like you should be the one getting married or you're so out of the loop that this will be the first time you lay eyes on the groom, you'll need to be at your best. The wedding weekend is the true test of a bridesmaid's mettle. Some get drunk and sneak off with the gorgeous guy from the catering crew. Others come to the rescue by racing back to the hotel to grab the good-luck locket the bride refuses to walk down the aisle without. For the final days and hours leading up to the wedding, you'll be on call, poised to spring into action at a moment's notice. Be nurturing and supportive with the bride. Be gracious with everyone from the florist to the groom's old summer camp buddy who talks your ear off because he doesn't know anyone else. Be observant. You're not here as an ornament; you're here to help. If you see something that needs doing, don't wait to be asked. Is the bride's grandma struggling to get up the front steps? Give her a hand. Has the pen for the guest book gone missing? Find another. Think of yourself as the person behind the scenes keeping the star happy and the show running smoothly.

CHECKLIST FOR CHECKING IN

Before the whirlwind of festivities gets under way, check in with the bride to see if she needs you to take care of any tasks at the wedding, such as:

- ❑ Transporting welcome baskets for guests to hotels
- ❑ Taking favors to reception site
- ❑ Taking birdseed/bubbles/rose petals to ceremony site or reception venue for showering of newlyweds and/or passing these items out to guests at the appropriate point
- ❑ Putting up signs directing guests to the reception room
- ❑ Placing baskets of amenities in the restrooms at reception venue
- ❑ Putting guest book and pens out and/or collecting them after the event
- ❑ Transporting flowers from ceremony site to reception and setting them up there
- ❑ Placing disposable cameras on tables and/or collecting them at end of event
- ❑ Pointing out important people to photographer and videographer
- ❑ Returning items to florist or cake designer
- ❑ Taking cake topper home or putting the top tier of the cake in freezer for the bride

Reflections from Real Brides

"I had each of my friends do what came most naturally to them. One picked out decorative hurricane lanterns with candles and set them up on the terrace, another put disposable cameras on the tables and encouraged people to use them, one served as a de facto director interacting with the service staff, and another just concentrated on keeping me sane.**"**
—Jeanne O'Brien-Coffey

Practice Makes Perfect: The Rehearsal

Usually held the day or evening before the wedding, the rehearsal is—as the name suggests—a trial run through the ceremony so that everyone knows what to do. Attendance is important to avoid glitches on the big day, so make every effort to be there. If you're traveling and won't be able to make it, ask another bridesmaid to pay close attention and pass all vital information on to you.

The Basics

Who attends? The entire wedding party, the parents of the bride and groom, the officiant, and anyone giving a reading, singing a song, or performing a special function in the ceremony participate in the rehearsal.

What should I wear? Attire varies from pearls and cocktail dresses to khakis and twin sets, depending on the ceremony venue and the type of rehearsal dinner being thrown afterward. If the rehearsal dinner will be very casual (a backyard barbecue, for instance), you may need to wear something dressier for the rehearsal and bring a change of clothes; check with the bride in advance.

Should I bring anything? If you've been entrusted with the ribbon bouquet from the shower, be sure to show up with it so the bride can hold it during the trial ceremony. If, as is usually the case, you'll be heading directly to the rehearsal dinner from the ceremony site, bring notes for any toast you plan to give. And make sure you've got directions to both sites—even if you're not the one driving.

Words to the Wise

※ Pay attention during the rehearsal. This is not the time to catch up with your long-lost high school pals or to worry about how bored your date looks slumped in the back pew waiting for you.

※ Make sure you know your cue for starting down the aisle during the processional, as well as whether you'll be paired up with a particular groomsman (or two if there's an uneven number) for the recessional.

※ Don't be embarrassed to ask questions if something seems unclear. The more comfortable you feel at the rehearsal, the more relaxed you'll be during the actual ceremony. The bride and groom may well be confused about certain steps themselves but feel too nervous or distracted to speak up. Don't assume the other bridesmaids understand what's going on and will be able to explain it to you later.

※ If you'll be giving a reading or performing a song, make sure you know where to stand, how to get there and back gracefully, and how to adjust the microphone to your height.

※ Familiarize yourself with the site layout. Where is the bridal suite? If there isn't one, where can you leave your purse and anything else you're carrying? Where are you supposed to stand before you walk down the aisle? Where are you supposed to go after the ceremony ends? Where is the nearest restroom (this is a good bit of knowledge to possess in case someone needs one at the last minute)?

※ If the bride has asked you to take care of certain details, such as putting a unity candle on the altar before the ceremony or taking a floral arrangement from the ceremony to the reception, discuss the logistics.

※ Do a quick check for potential hazards. If the aisle is slippery and you don't already have no-slip grips for the soles of your shoes, you might want to stop at a drugstore to pick some up. If it's oppressively hot, find out whether the air-conditioning will be on during the ceremony. If not and you'll be standing for a long service, determine whether there's a working drinking fountain nearby, or plan to bring a small bottle of chilled water (to be sipped before or after the ceremony—not during).

Message for the Maid of Honor

AT THE REHEARSAL, BE SURE TO REVIEW THE TIMING and logistics regarding any of the following that are applicable:

- The handoff and return of the bride's bouquet
- Holding the bride's gloves for her
- Lifting and repositioning the bride's veil (if she will be sipping from a wine goblet)
- Giving the groom's wedding band to the bride

However rare true love may be, it is less so than true friendship.
— François Duc de La Rochefoucauld

The Rehearsal Dinner

The rehearsal is almost always followed by a dinner attended by the happy couple, their parents, the wedding party and their dates, others taking part in the ceremony, and—sometimes—out-of-town guests or close relatives. Traditionally, the event is hosted by the groom's family, but these days anything goes (the bride's family might host, or the bride and groom themselves may be throwing the shindig). Rehearsal dinners run the gamut from fancy meals at chic restaurants to casual clambakes on the beach.

Party Pointers

※ Watch what you say during the rehearsal dinner. Some of the couple's relatives are bound to be in close proximity, and there's a good chance they'll overhear any cracks you make about the bride's bachelorette-party antics.

※ Watch your alcohol intake. Do you really want to end up with a wedding morning hangover that will leave your skin looking as green as your bridesmaid dress?

※ Aim to get home no later than 11:00 P.M., and try to make sure the bride does the same. Beauty rest is hard to come by as the wedding approaches, and you may be partying well into the wee hours the next night.

Toast of the Town

It's traditional for the hosts of the dinner to make a toast to the bride and groom and for the best man to say a few words as well. The engaged couple sometimes offers their own toast, too, thanking the hosts for all they've done and the guests for sharing in their celebration. As a bridesmaid, you may wish to raise a glass and say a few words in honor of the occasion. The bride may even ask you to do so. Rehearsal dinner toasts tend to be less formal than those given at wedding receptions; they can be anything from mushy, sentimental odes to humorous speeches sprinkled with anecdotes. Following are three rules to live by.

1. Keep your comments tame enough for the parents, grandparents, and officiant to hear.

2. Speak in only positive terms. Do not make disparaging remarks about anyone. Choose your words carefully, since what you consider to be good-natured ribbing might actually hurt someone's feelings or inadvertently spark a last-minute quarrel between the bride and groom. This is not the time to tell the man of the day—not to mention a roomful of people—that the bride thought he was a total geek when she first laid eyes on him.

3. Keep your toast short and sweet. If you ramble on until the guests are nodding off into their pepper-crusted salmon, people will probably avoid you like the plague the next day for fear that you'll talk their ear off (even if this result sounds like a good thing, be brief).

For more advice on composing and delivering a meaningful toast, see page 136.

Prep Work: Getting Ready on the Wedding Day

❋ Check the weather report before you leave home or the hotel. If precipitation is on the way, bring a hat, umbrella, raincoat, or anything else you might need.

❋ It's not a bad idea to check in with the bride to find out if there's anything she needs you to pick up on your way over.

❋ Before you walk out the door, make sure you have everything you need (review the tear-out Things to Bring checklist at the back of the book).

✻ Arrive at the appointed time. Don't show up a half hour early hoping to get a head start; you might interrupt the quiet breakfast that the bride planned with her mom and dad or those last few minutes she needs to review her vows.

✻ Be prepared to help the bride get dressed. Lacing up bodices and fastening all those tiny pearl buttons is often a two-woman job. Put her primping needs ahead of your own—it's her day.

✻ Remember to eat, and make sure the bride does, too. It's easy to get so busy that you forget all about food only to feel faint moments before the ceremony.

✻ Run any last-minute errands requested of you. If you'll have a car with you, be ready to roll at a moment's notice—your gas tank should be full, and if you're not from the area, you should have a map in your glove compartment.

✻ Make sure that you and the bride have everything you need before you leave her home or the hotel suite. If you're the maid of honor, check that you or the bride has the groom's wedding band stashed in a safe place.

✻ If you're the emotional type, likely to sob at the sight of your best friend from childhood saying "I do," tuck a tissue into the sleeve of your bridesmaid dress (make sure it's not peeping out) or fold one in the palm of your hand.

✻ Give the bride a gentle hug—being careful not to crush her dress or smudge her makeup—and tell her how beautiful she looks!

A Matter of Ceremony

✻ The way in which the processional takes place varies according to religion, formality, and the bride and groom's preferences. You'll probably walk down the aisle by yourself or side by side with another bridesmaid. If the bride has two honor attendants, they may walk together.

✻ The bride will most likely determine the order in which you walk and convey this information to you at the rehearsal. The maid of honor follows the other bridesmaids and stands closest to the bride during the ceremony. Many brides determine the order for the rest of the crew based on height. Do not get upset about where you fall in the lineup; the bride loves you all—that's why she asked you to play a special part in her special day.

※ For the recessional, you'll most likely follow the couple out in the opposite order you entered, starting with the maid of honor. As mentioned earlier, it's common to be paired up with a groomsman (or two) as you file out.

※ Stand up straight with your head held high and your shoulders back. You're aiming for elegant composure, not stiff-as-a-board rigidity—think prima ballerina, not West Point cadet.

※ Hold your bouquet with the handle securely in both hands. You should hold the bouquet just below waist level, angling your elbows out slightly so that the curve of your waistline is visible. (Many bridesmaids end up clutching their flowers to their chests, which results in a stiff, awkward look.)

※ Walk slowly, leaving a decent amount of space between you and the person in front of you; you should not be gaining on the person ahead of you. If you're in the lead, you'll need to make an extra effort to pace yourself.

※ If you're paired up with someone who seems to be engaged in a race to the finish, try to maintain a calm, even pace. Hopefully, he/she will take the hint.

※ Look straight ahead, even if you're fighting the desire to scan the crowd for a glimpse of your ex with his new girlfriend.

※ You don't have to smile if it makes you feel silly, but try to look pleasant. Make sure you're not scowling in concentration.

※ When you reach your destination (the officiant should have told you during the rehearsal where to stand), turn and look down the aisle to watch the bride approach.

※ Throughout the ceremony, keep your attention and your gaze fixed attentively on where the appropriate action is, be it on the couple, the officiant, or someone doing a reading. Don't say anything to the other attendants, smirk, or adjust your hair. Keep your bouquet in the same position as when you walked down the aisle.

※ There's no shame in dabbing your eyes during a moving ceremony; just don't blow your nose.

Message for the Maid of Honor

- When the bride arrives at the altar, huppah, or podium, check her train and veil and arrange them neatly as needed.

- If the bride will be sipping from a wine goblet during the ceremony, you may be expected to lift her veil and reposition it (this should be discussed during the rehearsal).

- Stay alert. Be poised to take the bride's bouquet when she's ready to hand it off. And when it's time for the ring exchange, present the groom's ring promptly to the bride. Don't wait for expectant glances and throat-clearing from everyone around you.

- After the bride and groom kiss, hand the bride's bouquet back to her (unless otherwise instructed) and straighten her train as she turns to face the guests for the recessional.

- If you've been asked to sign the marriage license after the ceremony, make sure you stick around to do so; don't disappear.

Say "Cheese"

- As a member of the wedding party, you'll almost certainly be expected to participate in a formal portrait photo session. Some couples schedule their formal portraits before the ceremony, while others slate them between the ceremony and reception. Still others do a portion of the photo shoot before the ceremony and the rest after.

- If the formal portraits will be taken after the ceremony, you'll miss a good portion of the cocktail hour (another good reason to make sure you eat something before the wedding). If you're bringing a date, warn him that he'll be left to fend for himself for a while.

✳ Your main duty during the photo session is to smile and cheerfully do whatever the photographer or the bride wants—no matter how ridiculous the pose may seem to you.

✳ Keep an eye on the bride's train and veil to make sure that they're arranged in a flattering way. And be prepared to hold any item that the bride wants to hand off—the bouquet, her wrap, etc.

✳ A videographer may tag along to capture a live version of the whole affair, so watch what you say.

THOUGHTFUL GESTURES FOR THE BRIDE

✳ Put together an emergency supply kit for the bride. Bring it to the location where the bride is getting dressed, the ceremony, and the reception. You can include:

- ❑ Needle and thread (the same color as bride's dress)
- ❑ Scissors
- ❑ Safety pins
- ❑ Headache medication and antacid tablets
- ❑ Blotting tissues
- ❑ Clear nail polish (for stocking runs)
- ❑ Bobby pins and hair spray
- ❑ Energy bar/granola bar and a bottle of water
- ❑ Breath fresheners
- ❑ Tweezers
- ❑ Dental floss/toothpicks
- ❑ Extra earring backs
- ❑ Stain remover
- ❑ Static-cling spray
- ❑ Fabric tape
- ❑ Eye drops

❋ When you arrive at the bride's home, bridal suite, or the beauty salon to help her get ready, surprise her with a treat—perhaps the three-berry scone and foam-free latte she loves from the corner bakery if it's morning, or a diet soda with lemon wedges and ice or another pick-me-up if it's afternoon.

❋ Bring a camera and take photos of everyone getting ready (especially if the professional photographer won't arrive until the ceremony). Capture the maid of honor helping the bride adjust the veil, the bridesmaids clustered around the mirror applying their lipstick, and other behind-the-scenes moments. Consider using black-and-white film for these early shots, then switching to color at the reception. This approach makes for a striking transition in a photo album.

❋ On the morning of the wedding, give the bride a card with a handwritten note expressing how much she means to you. Tell her how much you've enjoyed being able to share in her wedding, how happy you are for her, and that you wish her and the groom the very best. Try to do this before she's had her makeup done so that if she starts to cry, she won't have eyeliner or mascara running down her face (on that note, you may want to do it before you've put your makeup on, too).

❋ Purchase a frame with space for two photos facing each other. Put a picture of the bride with all of her bridesmaids on one side. Then find a quotation about friendship, and use a home computer to print it in an attractive font on decorative paper. Have the bridesmaids add their signatures around it in gold ink. Then cut it to size, and slip it into the other side of the frame.

❋ Bring a few tiny items that the bride can use as her something old, new, borrowed, and blue, in case she's missing anything. A few favorite blue options are a garter, a handkerchief, and blue nail polish (most brides use it on their toes—not their fingers).

Chapter Nine

The Reception

Champagne, canapés, cake, a chance to dance with that gorgeous grooms-man who flirted with you throughout the rehearsal dinner—generally speaking, the reception is one of the high points of your time as a bridesmaid. It's an opportunity to kick up your heels and join in some merrymaking as a reward for all of your hard work. That said, as a member of the wedding party, you still need to help out as needed. Make an effort to keep the guests mingling and the party hopping. Lead the charge to the dance floor if necessary. And be ready to assist the bride with anything she needs, from wrestling out of innumerable layers of tulle so she can use the ladies' room to helping the photographer identify impor-tant people who should be captured on film.

The Receiving Line

Purpose: The receiving line gives the happy couple and their parents the chance to put in a little personal face time with each and every guest. Members of the wedding party are sometimes called upon to participate in the receiving line as well; sometimes only the maid of honor is asked to join the lineup.

Place and time: This formal greeting of guests can take place right after the ceremony as guests exit the ceremony site or at the reception venue as guests enter.

Protocol: If you are asked to participate in the receiving line, smile, greet everyone graciously, shake hands, and introduce yourself to anyone you don't know. Do your best to keep the line moving. If you run into a long-lost friend, catch up later; don't hold up those still waiting, as they're probably eager to say hello to the couple and get to the bar. If someone else holds up the line and you find yourself struggling to make small talk with a complete stranger, explain how you know the bride and groom, and ask how this person knows the couple.

Pressing palms: If gloves are part of your ensemble, take them off and stash them somewhere safe. What to do with your bouquet? Either hold it in your left hand so you can shake with your right, or find a place to set it down.

Put on a brave face: The receiving line can feel awkward at times, especially when you don't know a lot of the guests. Just smile, be polite, and keep in mind that it will soon be over. Then you can reward yourself with a cosmopolitan and a crab puff.

Dancing the Night Away

❋ It's common for the bride and groom to ask just the members of the wedding party to take the dance floor for a song (or part of a song). Typically, the maid of honor partners with the best man, and the other bridesmaids pair up with the groomsmen. If you walked down the aisle with a guy, chances are you'll dance with him. Not sure? Ask the bride ahead of time.

❋ Unless there are a bunch of Fred and Ginger wannabes in the wedding party, you and your partner will probably default to the old stand-and-sway slow dance routine. If you feel self-conscious, remind yourself that everyone's eyes are on the newlyweds—not you—and take comfort in the fact that it won't last long. Bandleaders and deejays usually invite the other guests to join the wedding party on the dance floor before the song ends.

❋ Sometimes the groom will ask each of the bridesmaids for a dance during the reception. The groomsmen may do the same. If you are asked to dance by any of these men, you should graciously accept, even if you brought a date.

❋ Like it or not, bridesmaids are expected to dance. The idea is that you'll inspire others to get up and boogie. You're not obligated to spend every moment on the dance floor, but make a point to join in the fun. And be sure to participate in any group dances; you may have vowed not to do the Macarena or join a conga line unless your life depended on it, but put your principles on hold for the night.

Toasting Tips

※ Bridesmaids do sometimes give toasts at the wedding reception. If you'd like to say a few words at this event, check with the bride.

※ Toasting tends to take place after the guests take their seats, just before dessert, or, at a cocktails-only or buffet reception, after the receiving line disperses and the guests have their drinks in hand.

※ Find out where you'll stand to give your toast. If the wedding is large, you may need to walk to the stage or center of the dance floor and use the bandleader's microphone. If the wedding is small, you may be able to stand at your seat.

※ Unless you're a brilliant on-the-spot speaker with nerves of steel, determine what you'll say ahead of time. To alleviate the pressure during the hectic days and hours leading up to the wedding, start composing your toast several weeks in advance.

※ Personalize it. Mention how, where, and when you and the bride met; the first inkling you had that she and the groom were falling in love; and why you're sure they're made for each other. Share an anecdote or a favorite memory of the bride or the couple.

※ Stick to complimentary comments and G-ratings. Even good-natured ribbing or a passing reference to a love from long ago may upset someone.

※ Be sincere. Don't say anything you don't genuinely believe. If you hardly know the groom or you're not particularly fond of him, a toast about what a wonderful couple the newlyweds are and how crazy you are about them might sound forced. Focus your comments instead on your friendship with the bride and how delighted you are that she's found someone who makes her happy. Also mention what a beautiful wedding it is and what a good time everyone is having.

※ Finish off by congratulating the couple and wishing them well (don't forget to take a sip from your glass at the end).

※ If you're struggling to come up with eloquent wording, consider weaving in an inspiring quotation about marriage or love.

❋ Anticipate your emotions. Are you likely to burst into uncontrollable sobs at the thought of your best friend getting married? If so, a sentimental toast may choke you up so much you won't be able to get through it. Consider a more lighthearted tribute.

❋ Rehearse, rehearse, rehearse. The more time you spend practicing, the less nervous you'll be. Write your toast out and tape yourself reading it aloud or read it to a friend to make sure you're not speaking too fast. Stand when you practice.

❋ Keep it short and sweet—under two minutes. Try to build in a pause or two for effect. Time yourself when you practice to make sure you're not running long.

❋ Bring a written copy to the wedding. That way you'll be able to duck into the ladies' room and review it beforehand and/or refer to it during the actual toast. It's fine to glance at your notes as you speak; just don't keep your eyes fixed on them the whole time. Write in large clear letters that you'll be able to see easily, and use indelible ink that won't blur if a bit of champagne or a few tears spill on it. Use index cards if possible; notebook paper looks awkward, and microphones will pick up the sound of paper unfolding and crinkling.

❋ When you know the time for your toast is approaching, take deep breaths to keep yourself calm. Try to be conscious of breathing while you're giving your toast, too—it will help combat nervousness and prevent you from talking too fast.

❋ Watch your alcohol intake. A glass of champagne might be just what you need to bolster your confidence, but three or four might leave you slurring and swaying.

❋ Make eye contact as you speak. Look around the room at various guests, then turn to face the couple and raise your glass, addressing the end of the toast directly to them.

REFLECTIONS FROM REAL BRIDES

"My best friends from college all got together and wrote a lighthearted poem about me and my husband and read it aloud during our reception. It was better than any toast. It was a total surprise, and it made me laugh and remember just what good friends they were and how much they meant to me. It was especially great because they'd also known my husband for a long time, so they were able to relate the poem to both of us.**"**

—ALYSSA L. SHAFFER

Message for the Maid of Honor

AS USUAL, YOU'LL HAVE A FEW KEY RESPONSIBILITIES to handle. Chat with the bride a few days before the wedding to make sure you're clear about what you should expect and what she's expecting of you.

- If you'll be bustling her train, make sure you understand how to do it.
- Find out whether she'll need you to help with her dress when she uses the ladies' room.
- If she plans to change into a going-away outfit, ask whether she wants you to help her change or to take charge of packing up the wedding gown.

The Well-Behaved Bridesmaid: Etiquette Tips

※ Make an effort to mingle with guests at the reception; introduce them to one another, and talk to anyone who seems to be in need of a conversation partner.

※ Check with the bride regularly to find out if there's anything you can do to assist her.

※ Don't drink too much. Have fun, but stay in control. The bride might need your help with last-minute tasks. Plus, you don't want to embarrass her or her family.

Bouquet Toss Basics

※ If there's a bouquet toss and you're a single bridesmaid, you'll be expected to join the other unmarried female guests in this tradition. It is said that the lucky woman who catches the bouquet will be the next one married.

※ If you're mortified to join in or you find the whole tradition offensive, get over it for this one night. If you refuse to participate or force others to drag you into the mix kicking and screaming, you'll only make the bride feel bad.

※ If you're of the opposite mind-set and feel that you must be the one to catch those blooms, play fair. No pushing, tripping, or clawing others allowed.

※ The bouquet toss may be followed by a garter toss. The groom takes off the bride's garter and flings it at the single men; then the lucky recipient puts it on the leg of the woman who caught the bouquet. Hopefully, you'll be spared this particular humiliation.

Thoughtful Gestures for the Bride

❋ Find out whether the caterer can put together a pretty basket of edible treats for the couple to take with them when they leave the reception—a few of the hors d'oeuvres that travel well, mini-sandwiches made from the prime rib and rolls served at dinner, cookies from the dessert trays, and so on. Some caterers offer to do this as a matter of course, assuming brides and grooms will spend so much of the reception socializing with guests that they'll have little time to enjoy their own wedding meal.

❋ Sneak into the honeymoon suite, and sprinkle rose petals over the bed. Borrow a silver tray from room service, and leave champagne along with chocolate-covered strawberries, chilled milk and chocolate chip cookies, or some other treat for the newlyweds. (Talk with the front desk or the concierge about letting you into the room.)

❋ Put together a bon voyage basket for the couple to enjoy en route to their honeymoon. Include snacks, bottled water, sunscreen if they're going to the beach, massage oil, a mini–photo album with pictures arranged chronologically from the engagement party through the rehearsal dinner (get the most recent ones printed at a one-hour photo place), a CD of their favorite songs or tunes reflective of the honeymoon destination—whatever you think would enhance their trip. If you're really imaginative, you might even try your hand at creating a crossword tailored to their relationship (you can also order personalized crosswords via the Internet).

Afterword
Life Beyond the Wedding

During the long months of planning, it can seem like the wedding might never arrive. Then, before you know it, the day rushes by and you're waving so long as your newly married friend heads off into the sunset. What's next for you? This is the time to reward yourself for a job well done. You needn't splurge; even small treats and relaxation rituals can restore and rejuvenate. You may also use your newfound free time to extend one or two additional gestures of friendship to the bride. Sure, you've just spent countless hours proving what a devoted friend you are, but she may need your support now more than ever. It's not uncommon for brides to feel a sense of letdown once all the attention and activity surrounding the wedding have come and gone. Something as simple as a voice mail message or a cheerful note welcoming her home from the honeymoon and inviting her to lunch may help buoy her spirits if she's feeling low. What's more, such a gesture will reaffirm the strength of your friendship—for both of you.

Five Ways to Reward Yourself
for a Job Well Done

1. Get rid of your bridesmaid dress if you'll never wear it again. Give it to your niece to play dress-up in, have a seamstress make an evening bag out of the skirt fabric, or—better yet—donate it to charity. A number of organizations have been established in recent years in various cities across the country to collect gently used bridesmaid gowns and provide them to needy teens for prom wear. (To find out more, see these websites: princessproject.org; glassslipperproject.org; fairygodmothersinc.com.)

2. Go shopping and treat yourself to the most fabulous, flattering outfit you can find. (You deserve it after spending an entire day in that not-so-fabulous, not-so-flattering bridesmaid dress.) Plan a special occasion (a romantic dinner with your boyfriend, a night out dancing with the girls, a philharmonic performance) to give yourself an excuse to wear it.

3. Rejuvenate with a weekend of pampering to purge any residual wedding frazzle. Take a candlelit bubble bath. Give yourself a manicure. Go for long walks. Meditate. Stretch. Sleep.

4. Plan a vacation. (Why should the bride and groom be the only ones who get to enjoy a glamorous getaway?) Even if you won't be able to afford it for a few months, browse the travel section at local bookstores to decide where you want to go, and buy a guidebook or search online so you can start making concrete plans. Pick a date and place, and if you don't want to go solo, find a travel companion who shares your enthusiasm. Start marking down the days on a calendar and making a list of sites to visit, things to do, and new clothes to buy.

5. Give yourself a pat on the back. It might sound silly, but reprogramming negative internal messages of doubt and self-criticism with positive, reassuring ones can help raise your self-esteem and reduce your stress level. Make a written list of all the ways in which you came through for the bride. Write "congratulations" across the bottom of it. Then do something nice for yourself. Sign up for that

class you've been wanting to take, schedule a pampering spa day for yourself or give yourself a week off from housekeeping—you name it. You deserve it.

Preserving Your Friendship with the Bride

Sure, the dear friend whose wedding you've been involved in is the same person you've known for years, but marriage can alter the dynamics in female friendships. How much yours will change depends on your personality and lifestyle as well as hers. Do you get along with her husband? If you're married or in a relationship, how does your significant other feel about him? If you're single, will you feel like you're in the way? Are they comfortable having you around?

You may both need to make an effort to reestablish your relationship and find your footing. The same skills that served you well as a bridesmaid will prove indispensable now. Be open-minded, tolerant, and patient. Make a point to get together for girls' outings you can both enjoy. She may not want to hit the bars on Friday night, but you can still meet for a meal, a movie, or an afternoon of shopping. If she can't bear to part from her new hubby on the weekend, meet her for lunch during the week or keep in touch regularly by phone.

Follow-Up Touches for the Bride

1. Just before she returns from her honeymoon, leave a message on her answering machine welcoming her back and telling her what a wonderful time you had at the wedding. Tell her that everyone else is still raving about what a great event it was (every bride loves to hear that), and thank her for allowing you to play such an important role in it.

2. Get your film from the wedding printed, and send her copies so that they'll arrive shortly after she gets home from the honeymoon. Or e-mail her digital copies so that they're waiting for her when she returns. Bridal proofs can take months to arrive, and she'll be dying to see pictures from the big day.

3. Send her a thank-you note for the bridesmaid gift she gave you and for including you in her wedding.

4. Make a wedding scrapbook for her with copies of the photos you took and other keepsakes. Include a matchbook cover from the restaurant where the rehearsal was held, a postcard of the hotel where the wedding guests stayed, one of the decorative paper napkins from the reception, perhaps some pressed petals from your bouquet—anything that will be a treasured memento.

5. Invite her out for lunch, dinner, or drinks as soon as she gets back from her honeymoon. Make a toast to her happiness and to your continued friendship. If she's suffering from a postwedding letdown as lots of newly married women do, your attention will do wonders to raise her spirits.

REFLECTIONS FROM REAL BRIDES

"My sister (the maid of honor) made me a needlepoint picture of a bride and groom and my wedding date and had it beautifully framed. This was—and still is—one of the most precious gifts I've ever received."

—LOREN G. EDELSTEIN

Appendix

BRIDESMAID DRESS DESIGNERS

Many of the websites below feature highlights from designer collections, enable you to search for stores in your area carrying the designer's dresses, and provide information about upcoming trunk shows and sales.

Alexia Designs
www.alexiadesigns.com

Alfred Angelo Bridal
www.alfredangelo.com

Bill Levkoff
www.billlevkoff.com

David's Bridal
www.davidsbridal.com

The Dessy Group
www.dessy.com

J. Crew Wedding
www.jcrew.com/wedding.jsp

Jenny Yoo
www.jennyyoo.com

Jessica McClintock
www.jessicamcclintock.com

JLM Couture
www.jlmcouture.com

Siri
www.siriinc.com

Thread Design
www.threaddesign.com

Vera Wang Maids
www.verawang.com

Watters & Watters and WToo
www.watters.com

The Wedding Party
www.theweddingpartyonline.com

DRESS DEADLINES

Measurements: _____

Returned signed contract: _____

Deposit: _____

Balance: _____

First Fitting: _____

Second Fitting: _____

QUESTIONS TO ASK: SITE MANAGER OF PARTY VENUE

※ Do you have a private room? If not, is there something you can do to create some privacy for our group?

※ Where would we be seated?

※ How would the tables be set up?

※ Is there a time limit? What happens if we exceed the allotted time? What are the overtime charges?

※ What are the menu choices?

※ Is it possible to accommodate special dietary needs?

※ Can we bring in a cake from an outside bakery?

※ What are the fees, and what's included?

※ Are drinks included, and if so, what types (soft drinks, coffee and tea, alcohol)?

※ Is it possible to limit the alcoholic beverages to a single type of cocktail?

※ Can we bring in our own champagne or wine, and if so, is there a corkage fee?

※ Are gratuities included?

※ Is there a minimum requirement or a maximum head count allowed? When will you need a final number?

※ Will we have our own wait staff?

※ Do you supply any table decorations or background music? Can we bring our own?

※ If we bring our own music, are you equipped to play it?

※ How far in advance can we arrive to start decorating and setting up?

※ Does the venue have liability insurance?

※ What is the payment policy?

※ What is the cancellation policy?

QUESTIONS TO ASK: CATERER

※ What are the menu choices?

※ Is it possible to accommodate special dietary needs?

※ Are ingredients commonly responsible for allergic reactions (such as peanut oil) noted?

※ Is there a minimum requirement in terms of head count or dollars?

※ Do you provide beverages, and if so, what are our options?

※ What are the fees for the things we are interested in?

※ Do you deliver, or will we need to pick up the food? Is there a delivery fee?

※ What is the timing for delivery/pickup?

※ Will the food be ready to serve, or will some preparation work be involved on our part? How much?

※ Will you set up on-site? If so, is there an additional fee?

※ Do you provide wait staff to serve the food or attend the buffet as needed? Will the wait staff clean up as well? If so, what are the fees?

※ Will we need any special equipment?

※ Will we need to return serving dishes? If so, which ones and by what date?

※ What is the name and phone number of the person who would be our contact on the day of the event?

※ Do you have liability insurance?

※ What are the payment terms?

※ What is the cancellation policy?

※ Do you have references?

QUESTIONS TO ASK: RENTAL COMPANY

✳ Do you have a minimum requirement in terms of number of items rented?

✳ Do you deliver, or will we need to pick up the items?

✳ If we'll need to pick up the rentals, how heavy are they? How many women will be needed to carry them? Can your staff help load them into our car?

✳ How early can the rentals be delivered/picked up?

✳ Are we responsible for returning the items, or will you retrieve them? What is the time frame for this?

✳ Are there late fees, and when do they go into effect?

✳ Are there any requirements regarding the return of the items?

✳ Are there any special handling or cleaning instructions? If so, will you provide written instructions?

✳ Do you have a catalog or in-store samples of the various styles we can choose from?

✳ What are the fees for the rental items we're interested in?

✳ Do these fees include setup? If not, what are the setup fees?

✳ Are there any additional fees?

✳ What happens if we break something?

✳ Do you have liability insurance?

✳ What is your payment policy?

✳ What is your cancellation policy?

✳ Is there an emergency contact for the day of the shower in case the delivery doesn't arrive or something malfunctions?

Index

PERSONAL WEDDING DIRECTORY

Bridesmaid #1

Name: _____

Address: _____

_____

_____

Phone: (H)_____ (C)_____

(O)_____

E-mail: _____

Wedding day contact #: _____

How she knows the bride: _____

Other notable information: _____

_____

_____

Bridesmaid #2

Name: _____

Address: _____

_____

_____

Phone: (H)_____ (C)_____

(O)_____

E-mail: _____

Wedding day contact #: _____

How she knows the bride: _____

Other notable information: _____

_____

_____

Bridesmaid #3

Name: _____

Address: _____

_____

_____

Phone: (H)_____(C)_____

(O)_____

E-mail: _____

Wedding day contact #: _____

How she knows the bride: _____

_____

Other notable information: _____

_____

_____

Bridesmaid #4

Name: _____

Address: _____

_____

_____

Phone: (H)_____(C)_____

(O)_____

E-mail: _____

Wedding day contact #: _____

How she knows the bride: _____

_____

Other notable information: _____

_____

_____

Bridesmaid #5

Name: _____

Address: _____

_____

_____

Phone: (H)_____(C)_____

(O)_____

E-mail: _____

Wedding day contact #: _____

How she knows the bride: _____

Other notable information: _____

_____

_____

Bridesmaid #6

Name: _____

Address: _____

_____

_____

Phone: (H)_____(C)_____

(O)_____

E-mail: _____

Wedding day contact #: _____

How she knows the bride: _____

Other notable information: _____

_____

_____

Bridesmaid #7

Name: _____

Address: _____

_____

_____

Phone: (H)_____(C)_____

(O)_____

E-mail: _____

Wedding day contact #: _____

How she knows the bride: _____

_____

Other notable information: _____

_____

_____

Mother of the Bride

Name: _____

Address: _____

_____

_____

Phone: (H)_____(C)_____

(O)_____

E-mail: _____

_____

Stepmother of the Bride

Name: _____

Address: _____

_____

_____

Phone: (H)_____(C)_____

(O)_____

E-mail: _____

Groom

Name: _____

Address: _____

_____

_____

Phone: (H)_____(C)_____

(O)_____

E-mail: _____

Source of Bridesmaid Dress

Store name: _____

Address: _____

_____

_____

Contact person: _____

Phone: _____

E-mail: _____

Beauty Salon (for prewedding hair/makeup appointments)

Stylist's name: _____

Salon name: _____

Address: _____

_____

_____

Phone: _____

Hotel

Name: _____

Address: _____

_____

_____

Phone: _____

Reservation code: _____

Confirmation #: _____

One stress-relieving activity of your choice
(manicure, pedicure, walk in the park,
or tea and sympathy)

Complimentary transportation provided

One girls' night out with all the trimmings
(margaritas and tequila shots included)

One girls' night in with all the trimmings
(movies and double-cheese
pizzas included)

Wedding Day Checklist: Things to Bring

Use this checklist on the day of the wedding to make sure you don't forget anything.

- ❏ Button-down shirt for beauty appointment
- ❏ Bridesmaid dress
- ❏ Shoes
- ❏ Jewelry
- ❏ Gloves
- ❏ Wrap
- ❏ Bra/underpinnings
- ❏ Panty hose (bring an extra pair)
- ❏ Evening bag
- ❏ Invitation
- ❏ Directions to ceremony and reception
- ❏ Camera
- ❏ Camera charger or extra camera batteries
- ❏ Cell phone (make sure it's off during ceremony and reception)
- ❏ Wedding-day contact numbers for other bridesmaids, the bride, and any other key players
- ❏ Cash and credit card
- ❏ Facial tissues
- ❏ Blotting tissues
- ❏ Makeup and makeup remover (to fix tear-induced smudges)
- ❏ Bobby pins
- ❏ Travel-size hairspray
- ❏ Small brush and/or comb

(continued on back)

- ❑ Breath fresheners (leave the chewing gum at home)
- ❑ Travel-size dental floss
- ❑ Compact mirror
- ❑ Sewing needle, thread the color of your dress, and small pair of scissors (for quick mends)
- ❑ Safety pins
- ❑ Watch (tuck it into your purse if you don't want to wear it)
- ❑ Any allergy medication or prescription medication you'll need
- ❑ Headache relief
- ❑ Antacid tablets
- ❑ Clear adhesive bandages (in case those new shoes give you blisters)
- ❑ Rewetting eye drops (if you wear contacts)
- ❑ Tampons
- ❑ Clear nail polish for runs in stockings
- ❑ Colored nail polish for touchups to manicure
- ❑ Nail file
- ❑ Sunscreen (if ceremony or reception will be held outdoors)
- ❑ Card for bride, with a special note written inside (optional)
- ❑ Any items you're supplying for "something old, something new, something borrowed, something blue"
- ❑ Copy of reading you're giving or solo you're singing at ceremony, if applicable
- ❑ Written copy of your toast (if you plan to make one)
- ❑ Groom's ring, if you've already been entrusted with it
- ❑ Emergency kit for bride (optional; see page 131)
- ❑ Anything bride has asked you to bring